stress-free
Family Meal Planning

Easy, Healthy Recipes *for* Busy Homes

Kristen McCaffrey

Founder *of* Slender Kitchen

PAGE STREET
PUBLISHING CO.

PAGE STREET
PUBLISHING CO.

First published in 2020 by
Page Street Publishing Co.
27 Congress Street, Suite 105
Salem, MA 01970
www.pagestreetpublishing.com

Distributed by Macmillan, sales in Canada by The Canadian Manda Group.

24   23   22   21   20   1   2   3   4   5

ISBN-13: 978-1-64567-022-3
ISBN-10: 1-64567-022-8

Library of Congress Control Number: 2019951538

Cover and book design by Rosie Stewart for Page Street Publishing Co.
Photography by Becky Winkler

Printed and bound in China

Dedication

To all the Moms, Dads, and caretakers who thanklessly get dinner on the table night after night. Thank you. You are the inspiration for this book.

To my own family, who inspires me daily to get creative in the kitchen and find joy in meal time. I love you.

Table of Contents

Welcome   7

Introduction   7

My Story   7

What "Healthyish" Means   9

Why Meal Planning Matters   11

Why Meal Plan   11

Meal Planning Myths   12

Becoming a Master Meal Planner   15

How to Use This Book   15

Before You Start Planning   16

Using the Meal Plans   18

Grocery Shopping Tips   20

Food Storage and Safety   22

Meal Prep and Kitchen Hacks   24

Week 1   29

Weekly Calendar   30

Shopping List   31

Game Plan   32

Zucchini Banana Bread Baked Oatmeal   35

Turkey Bacon and Spinach Breakfast Sandwiches   36

Blueberry-Banana Greek Yogurt Pancakes   39

Barbecue Chicken "Empanadas"   40

Slow Cooker Mediterranean Beef with Tzatziki   43

Israeli Salad   44

One-Pot Creamy Sausage and Pepper Pasta   47

Cashew Chicken and Pineapple Fried Rice   48

Baked Pizza Pork Chops with Cauliflower   51

Crispy Herb Polenta Fries   52

Skillet Turkey Enchiladas   55

One-Pan Honey Mustard Salmon, Potatoes, and Broccoli   56

Cheddar-Apple Chicken Burgers   59

Potato Zucchini Muffin Tots   60

Week 2   63

Weekly Calendar   64

Shopping List   65

Game Plan   66

Pepperoni Pizza Mini Frittatas   69

Pumpkin–Chocolate Chip Muffins   70

Ultimate Breakfast Scramble   73

Mason Jar Instant Lasagna Soup   74

Slow Cooker Honey-Soy Chicken   77

Coconut Quinoa   78

Spicy Asian Brussels Sprouts   81

Creamy Spinach and Artichoke Pasta   82

Broiled Barbecue Flank Steak with Mango Salsa   85

Cilantro-Lime Cauliflower Rice and Beans   86

Skillet Pork Tenderloin with Apples and Snap Peas   89

Sheet-Pan Pesto Meatballs, Roasted Tomatoes, and Gnocchi   90

Tomato-Basil Fish 93

Lemon-Garlic Roasted Broccoli and Polenta 94

Crispy Baked Sweet Potato Taquitos 97

Mexican Fruit Salad 98

Week 3 101

Weekly Calendar 102

Shopping List 103

Game Plan 104

Ham, Cheese, and Zucchini Breakfast Quesadillas 107

Cinnamon Apple and Pear Oatmeal 109

Sheet-Pan Sweet Potato and Veggie Breakfast Hash 110

Crunchy Thai Peanut and Mango Salad 113

Slow Cooker Four-Veggie Lasagna 114

Italian Chopped Salad 117

Creamy Ranch Chicken Bites 118

Roasted Ranch Butternut Squash and Asparagus 121

Sheet-Pan Sausage, Potatoes, Peppers, and Onions 122

Mini Meatloaves and Green Beans 125

Garlic Sweet Potato Wedges 126

Sesame-Orange Chicken and Broccoli 129

Blackened Fish Tacos with Mexican Corn Slaw 130

Shortcut Refried Beans 133

Chickpea Pizza 134

Simply Yogurt Caesar Salad 137

Week 4 139

Weekly Calendar 140

Shopping List 141

Game Plan 142

Pesto and Cherry Tomato Frittata 145

Apple-Cinnamon Granola 146

Blueberry-Maple Breakfast Sausage 149

Cheesy Broccoli and Cauliflower Chowder 150

Slow Cooker Citrus Carnitas with Pineapple Salsa 153

Cowboy Caviar 154

One-Pot American Chop Suey 157

Crispy Coconut Chicken Strips 158

Sesame-Mandarin Green Beans 161

Asian Peanut Lettuce Wraps 162

Sweet and Spicy Pepper Jelly Chicken and Cauliflower 165

Shrimp Scampi Cakes 166

Crispy Garlic Squash Fries 169

Sloppy Joe–Stuffed Sweet Potatoes 170

Bonus Recipes 172

Fancy Toast Five Ways 173

Creamy Chocolate Smoothie 174

Italian Baked Eggs 175

Build-Your-Own Chicken Salad 176

Turkey Sausage and Tortellini Soup 177

"Steak" and Cheese–Stuffed Zucchini 178

Slow Cooker Salsa Chicken Chili 179

Baked Cilantro-Lime Salmon Packets 180

Sheet-Pan Chicken and Vegetable Stir-Fry 181

Beyond the Book 182

Acknowledgments 185

About the Author 185

Index 186

Welcome

Introduction

If there is one thing you can do to make your kitchen life easier and less stressful, meal planning is the answer every time.

Ask me almost any question about how to eat healthier, save money on groceries, stop stressing about what's for dinner, and learning to cook, and my answer will always be meal planning. To say I am obsessed with meal planning barely scratches the surface. Meal planning truly is the thing that will make the biggest impact on your health, budget, stress level, and cooking skills.

With that said, the most important reason you should start meal planning is to enjoy mealtime again. Feeding your family should feel good. It should bring *joy*. But for too many of us, that's just not the case.

Mealtimes can bring feelings of stress, guilt, and frustration. With hectic schedules and busy lives, mealtime moved from a special time to connect with our families to another task on an ever growing to-do list.

I am here to tell you that meal planning will break that cycle. Meal planning makes it possible to get a healthy meal on the table night after night. Meal planning changes the daily mealtime battle. Instead of staring into the fridge every night, hoping for an answer, you will go home knowing what's for dinner, knowing you have everything you need to make it, and knowing your family will have that precious time to be together.

My Story

I come from a long line of women who love to cook and somehow do it effortlessly. While I was growing up, my mom got dinner on the table every single night—between a full-time job, three kids, and endless activities. To her, that time was sacred family time. Whether it was 9:00 p.m. after a soccer game or we had three extra friends squeezed around the table, we were eating a home-cooked meal every night.

Now, with two kids of my own, I have no idea how she did it. She was just one of those people who naturally made it happen. Unfortunately, that's not me. The gift of effortlessly whipping up meal after meal was not one I inherited. I have to work at it.

However, this story and my love of meal planning actually started with my struggle to lose weight, eat well, and find a healthy and happy balance in my own life.

If I look back 10 years, I was 30 pounds (14 kg) overweight and I knew how to cook exactly one dish that didn't come directly from my freezer. I was tired. I was uncomfortable in my body. Quite honestly, I was exhausted after years of trying diet after diet without any long-term success and felt far from my best.

Deep down, I knew something needed to change. I was done with not feeling like myself. I was done with always being tired and having no energy. I was done with throwing myself into another quick-fix solution that ultimately didn't work. I was done with constantly trying to camouflage myself. It was time to make a real change.

That's when I found meal planning. After talking to countless friends and family who had either successfully lost weight or simply lived a balanced, healthy lifestyle, I learned two things that would change my approach to food and eating forever: It was time to learn to cook, and it was time to start planning my meals.

Following the advice of my aunt—"If you can read, you can cook"—I devoured blogs, cookbooks, magazines, and videos. With each healthy recipe I followed, I grew more confident in the kitchen. I also started meal planning. Each week I sat down on Sunday and planned my meals for the week. I built shopping lists, adjusted serving sizes, and got organized for the week.

It worked. Over the course of the next year, I lost a total of 35 pounds (16 kg). More importantly, I started to feel good again. I gained energy, confidence, and freedom—freedom from the negative thoughts, constant stress about what to eat, and battle to simply feel good.

And that's what brings us to this book. These days I have two little girls and life is busier than ever. It would have been easy to throw everything I learned to the side, but instead I find myself relying on meal planning more than ever. It saves my sanity.

I hope this book can do the same for you. This book takes the hard work out of meal planning and getting a healthy dinner on the table. Instead of spending every Sunday looking for recipes and building shopping lists, you can turn to this book and follow a weekly menu full of healthy meals that taste good, are easy to prepare, and can make mealtime enjoyable again.

I couldn't be more excited to start this meal planning journey with you! So grab your calendar—let's make dinnertime stress-free, delicious, and joyful.

What "Healthyish" Means

Feeding a family is hard work, especially when you are trying to eat healthfully. While I realize that looks different in every family, after some time, I have landed on my personal healthy-eating philosophy. Let's call it "healthyish."

I could write an encyclopedia about what this concept means, but at its core, it's simple. It's also something that resonates with most parents I know: If I can get my kids to happily eat a recipe packed with fruits, veggies, whole grains, and lean proteins, I will happily add some melted cheese, chocolate chips, or ketchup.

That's really it. All the recipes in this book strive to use lots of fresh produce, lean proteins, healthy fats, as well as whole grains, legumes, nuts, and seeds. (Just look at the shopping lists.) But you will also find pasta and cheese and chocolate chips. It's all about balance and moderation.

To break it down further, here's what healthyish looks like for my family:

- Always choose real food over processed when possible.

- Focus on balanced meals that include a lean protein, whole grain, fruits and/or veggies, and healthy fats.

- Try and include fruits and/or veggies in every single meal.

- Use natural, unrefined sweeteners (e.g., pure maple syrup and honey) over refined sugar as much as possible.

- Cook one meal to feed the whole family. (I'm speaking to mental health here!) If needed, get creative about how it is served.

- Cook food that works for your family and lifestyle. No guilt.

- Eat food that gives you energy and makes you feel good.

- Don't worry about the occasional treat, restaurant meal, and splurge. Food should be fun! Everything in moderation.

Why Meal Planning Matters

Why Meal Plan

You bought this book, so you are already excited about meal planning. Yet, all too often, we start out with the best intentions and then life happens. Consider this section your extra push.

Here's why meal planning will fundamentally change your life in the kitchen:

- **Meal planning helps you eat healthier.** It's easy to say we want to eat healthier, but then hunger strikes and we reach for what we are used to. If you really want to change your habits and get healthy, you have to have a plan for your meals. And they better taste good. Armed with a meal plan, you'll avoid sugary snacks, processed convenience food, takeout, and other unhealthy choices.

- **Meal planning helps you save money.** Most of us go to the grocery store without a list and without a plan. Get organized before you go to the store and you won't waste money buying things you don't need. It's that simple.

- **Meal planning helps you reduce waste.** It's estimated that between 30 and 40 percent of the food produced in the United States becomes food waste. That's 1 pound (450 g) of food per day per person. Not only is that expensive but it's not great for the environment either. When you go to the store with a shopping list based on the recipes and foods you are going to eat, you can greatly reduce the amount of food you waste.

- **Meal planning helps you learn to cook.** My aunt Joanie famously says, "If you can read, you can cook." I couldn't agree more. The easiest way to learn to cook is to get in the kitchen. Cooking a variety of dishes every week with different proteins, produce, and techniques will teach you to cook. You'll build confidence, understand how flavors work together, and pick up new skills.

- **Meal planning helps you avoid getting bored.** Without a well-laid plan, most of us see a recipe that makes our mouth water but then we end up making the same thing again and again and again. Food should be fun and exciting. No one wants to eat chicken breast and steamed broccoli every night.

- **Meal planning helps you reduce stress.** Imagine a world where, every single night, you could confidently answer the question, "What's for dinner?" Your fridge and pantry are stocked with all the ingredients you need. There's no need for last-minute trips to the grocery store. You've got a recipe ready to go that tastes good, is easy to prepare, and is actually good for you.

- **Meal planning helps you learn to love mealtime again.** The single most important thing that meal planning can do is help you fall back in love with mealtime. Cooking and nourishing your family feels good and with a plan, mealtime becomes something you look forward to every day.

Meal Planning Myths

To be honest with you, the first few times you sit down to make a meal plan and use it, it's going to be hard. This book will make it infinitely easier since it provides all the recipes and shopping lists, but there is still a mental leap most of us will have to make.

Whether or not we realize it, there are probably some mental blocks that have stopped us from meal planning in the past. So instead of ignoring them, let's get them out in the open and talk about how to overcome them.

"I Don't Have Time."
This is the most common objection I hear when it comes to meal planning: "I don't have time to look for recipes, to write out a shopping list, to create a menu."

I would argue that you don't have the time *not* to meal plan. The mental energy you expend daily trying to figure out what to eat for breakfast, lunch, and dinner takes time. The mental energy it takes to figure out what you need and what's already in the fridge. The 30 minutes it takes to decide where to order takeout and what to get. The time it takes to pick it up. The time you spend beating yourself up because you ordered takeout, ate convenience food, or reached for something that didn't make you feel good. All of these things take up more time than it will take you to use the plans in this book and eventually create your own.

"It's Too Expensive to Eat Healthy and Meal Plan."
The first few times you do all your grocery shopping on one day and begin to stock your pantry with healthy essentials, it may feel expensive. After the first couple of weeks, most people find they actually save money—a lot of money—when they stop buying things they don't need and splurging on takeout and convenience food.

"It's Too Much Work."
I will admit that the first time you sit down to meal plan on your own, it feels like a lot of work. You have to search for recipes, adjust the recipes, and build a shopping list. (Luckily, I did all that hard work for you.)

Meal planning can take 2 to 3 hours when you first start out. That's a lot of weekend time to give up. (Again, unless you are smart and let someone—*wink*—do it for you.)

However, let's think about the time you spend when you don't meal plan. You might spend 15 to 30 minutes daily looking at recipes and thinking about what to make. You may spend another 30 minutes daily stopping at the grocery store to grab what you need.

By the end of the week, you have probably spent 6 to 8 hours just thinking about and planning for your nightly dinner. And we aren't even talking about breakfast and lunch.

Meal planning saves times when you do it right.

"My Family Is Too Picky."

After people tell me they don't have the time, the next thing I hear is that their family is too picky. That they could never make just one meal to feed their whole family. My response: For your own mental health and clarity, you have to do this. Unless you are a short-order cook, you just don't have the time and mental space to cook multiple meals every night.

Instead, it's time to get creative. We had two rules when it came to mealtime in our house as I was growing up: You have to try it, and you have to eat your vegetables. Today in my own house, I follow those rules religiously.

I also get creative. There are so many ways to manipulate and adapt a meal to make it friendlier to a picky eater. Deconstruct it. Serve it in a different way. Start small. Focus on the familiar.

Throughout this book, I will provide tips and ideas for making recipes kid-friendly and picky eater–friendly. However, I recommend pushing your kid to try new things. Expose them to flavors, model positive eating, and, if needed, have a healthy backup.

"What If I Am Not in the Mood?"

I can't tell you how many times that meal planning falls apart because someone isn't in the mood for what's on the schedule. There are a few ways to fight this:

- **Check in.** First, check in and see if you truly aren't in the mood. Many times when I am not in the mood, I am actually just tired and don't feel like cooking. Once I realize that, I almost always can find some extra motivation to get in the kitchen.

- **Be flexible.** If you schedule pasta for Wednesday but just don't feel like it, cook what you had planned for Thursday or Friday instead of abandoning your plan.

- **Let yourself off the hook.** As long as it isn't happening every night, it's okay to let yourself off the hook sometimes. If you really don't want to eat something, throw the protein in the freezer and eat something else. One night off plan isn't going to ruin anything. It is only a problem if it's happening every night.

- **Get creative.** Another option when you aren't in the mood is to switch things up. If you were planning on making a pasta dish with ground beef but feel like burgers, just make burgers. Store the pasta, turn the ground beef into burger patties, and make the same side dish. Nothing is wasted, and everyone is happy.

Becoming a Master Meal Planner

How to Use This Book

In this book, you will find four weeks of full meal plans with recipes for breakfast, lunch, and dinner (or leftovers). You'll also find shopping lists, weekly meal prep ideas, and daily strategies for making mealtime as easy as possible. It's everything you need to feed your family three healthy meals daily for the next month.

Yet since every home is different, I know it's not possible to simply grab this book and run to the grocery store. You'll want to make adjustments based on your family size, schedule, and preferences. Meal planning only works when it is built around your needs.

This book is set up with that in mind. Making changes and adapting these meal plans to your needs is easy. With a few minutes of prep work, you can have your exact meal plan set up and ready to go.

Additionally, I offer a digital tool that will do all of this for you in just a few clicks. With it, you can change the number of servings, eliminate recipes from the meal plans, add new recipes, and more.

Digital Companion

To make things easy, all of the meal plans in this book are available to print at https://www.slenderkitchen.com/cookbook/redeem.

In addition, you'll find a digital version of the meal planner that will automatically adjust the recipes to the servings you need. Simply enter your needs, and it will give you a tailored meal plan ready to go.

Before You Start Planning

To truly make a meal plan work, you have to start by doing a little bit of preplanning. Here are the questions to ask yourself before diving into the meal plans.

What Is Your Schedule for the Week?

This is the number one question you need to ask yourself before meal planning. You need to think through each family member and all the different activities and needs they will have that week.

Are you going out to dinner at all? How many people will be eating each meal? Will you be particularly busy one night and need something quick? Will you be out one night and need something that can be prepped ahead of time?

This type of thinking will help you tailor the meal plan for your needs. It is what makes the meal plan actually work.

Without a doubt, consulting my schedule is the most important thing I do every week before meal planning. It helps me realize when I need to plan an easy dinner for our sitter because we have a date night, or when I need to cook extra servings so we can take the leftovers to the office. It also ensures I don't waste food buying ingredients for a meal that we won't actually eat.

Is There Anything You Need to Use Up?

There is nothing worse than throwing food away. I joke that it is like lighting money on fire. For that reason, I am always trying to minimize food waste by starting with my fridge, freezer, and pantry.

Perhaps we missed a meal the week before due to an impromptu dinner out, so I will want to use those ingredients up as soon as possible. Maybe there is some soup in the freezer that needs to be eaten. Or it could be that your pantry is overflowing and you just want to use up some of your stockpile.

When this happens, plan a meal around those ingredients that you need to use up.

What Are Your Family's Needs and Preferences?

Most of the time, we inherently know our loved ones' needs and preferences, but the topic is still worth mentioning. Before I start meal planning, I always ask myself if there is anything specific I need to be considering when looking at this week's menu.

Keep these considerations in the back of your mind when you look over the weekly meal plan. It doesn't mean you will automatically change or eliminate a meal, but it will help you get creative in thinking about how to use the meal for your home and if there are any small adjustments you need to make.

Common Scenarios

If you're wondering how to adjust the number of servings based on your family's unique needs, following are some common scenarios and tips on how to handle them:

- **Family of five:** Most families find that tripling the recipes works best. The extra serving almost always gets eaten during the meal or the next day.

- **Four for dinner, one for breakfast and lunch:** We find this situation is fairly common, but it makes meal planning a little tricky. Here's what to do:

  - Cut the servings for breakfast recipes in half. This will give you enough for one person all week.

  - Prepare the Sunday lunch and dinner options as written. Eat the Sunday lunch leftovers Tuesday, Thursday, and Friday. Eat the Sunday night dinner leftovers Monday and Wednesday. Wing it for lunch on Saturday based on what is left in the fridge.

  - Make all dinners for four people. That means doubling the ones with 2 servings and leaving the ones with 4 servings as they are.

  - Don't forget to adjust the shopping list as needed.

- **Extra-hungry family of four:** Triple the recipe so you have 2 extra servings for each meal. This is usually enough to make everyone happy.

Using the Meal Plans

The meal plans in this book are set up to make them as easy as possible to personalize. From the number of servings to creating a guide to quickly matching recipes to the shopping list, this is a book that's meant to be used. Mark up the pages, make notes, and don't be afraid to get it dirty.

Servings

One of the hardest things about writing a meal planning book is trying to figure out how many servings to include for each recipe. Not only are there tons of different household sizes out there, but there are also different needs for different meals. Maybe you need a recipe for four for dinner but you're only feeding two for lunch. It could be that you have some hungry folks at home who need more than one portion. Needs vary home to home.

After speaking to countless readers, I decided to create the meal plans with a base of two servings. Starting with two servings makes the math easy, mostly. Have a family of four? Double it. Need some recipes for one? Cut them in half. Have a family of five? Triple it (between everyone, the extra portion will get eaten).

However, I also wanted to provide an option for those who want something more exact and that's why I have a digital companion that will do this for you. Visit https://www.slenderkitchen.com/cookbook/redeem. Simply enter your needs and the digital companion will calculate the exact amount of servings you need for each recipe and build your shopping list. Easy-peasy.

Leftovers

In our world, it is almost impossible to cook a new recipe for breakfast and lunch every day. And—let's be honest—who wants to? For that reason, we rely heavily on leftovers to fulfill our weekly breakfast and lunch needs.

Every week, you will find the same breakfasts used Sunday, Tuesday, and Thursday as well as Monday, Wednesday, and Friday. You'll also find the same recipe used Sunday and Tuesday for lunch. Then throughout the week, we will strategically use leftovers from dinner to make our lunches.

A quick note about servings. As I mentioned, all the meals are built around two servings. This includes leftovers. There will be enough for two servings of leftovers. For example, a meal that will be used twice for leftovers, like the Sunday night slow cooker meals, will yield six servings total. Same for breakfast.

If you will need a different number of leftovers, you will want to adjust the recipe (or use the digital companion, which is the easiest option).

The System

After countless years of creating meal plans, I found that the easiest way to help readers adjust the meal plan is to include a quick key to match the ingredients in the shopping list to their corresponding recipes.

You will notice that each recipe in the meal plans includes a letter in parentheses. Each of those letters corresponds to the respective ingredients in the shopping list. That way, if you need to change something, just look for the corresponding letter in the shopping list. Then you can easily change the amount, eliminate ingredients, or make any other necessary adjustments.

Putting It All Together

Remember all that thinking you did in the preplanning stage? Now it is time to put it to use. Here's what to do:

- **Eliminate any meals you don't need.** Start by removing any meals you won't need. Going out to dinner on Friday? It's time to delete that meal and its ingredients. See something you don't like? Let's get rid of it like so:

    - Find the meal and corresponding letters in the weekly calendar for the meal you don't need.

    - Check to see if the meal plan includes leftovers from that meal. Decide if you still want to cook the meal for the leftovers or eliminate it completely. Adjust the number of servings if you still want the leftovers.

    - Pull out the shopping list and find all the ingredients with the same letter. Eliminate that ingredient or reduce the amount if it is an ingredient used in more than one recipe.

    - Repeat the preceding steps as needed.

- **Add new meals.** Now it's time to add any new recipes you may want to prepare. Follow these steps:

    - Take a minute to decide how many servings you will need, taking leftovers into account if you want them.

    - Add the necessary ingredients to your shopping list.

- **Adjust the serving sizes.** Look back to the weekly schedule you created and adjust the serving sizes as needed. Scale the recipe up or down and adjust the corresponding ingredients in the shopping list. Or let us do this for you in the digital companion.

- **Add items to your shopping list.** Now it's time to add anything else you may need to your weekly shopping list (snacks, drinks, school lunch items, household items, and so on).

Here is an example to help bring it all together:

Carol has a family of four people. She will be preparing only breakfast and lunches for her and her spouse. Her kids tend to eat the same things for breakfast and eat lunch at school. On Friday, Carol's family is going out to dinner and on Saturday she is having four extra guests for dinner.

Here's how Carol would adjust her meal plan:

- Carol eliminates the Friday night meal and adjusts the shopping list. She decides to wing it for lunch and make do with what's in the fridge, so she also eliminates the leftovers from that meal that were supposed to be lunch on Saturday.

- Carol adjusts the servings for Saturday night dinner to eight people. This means quadrupling the recipe and updating the shopping list to reflect that change.

- Carol adds breakfast items to the shopping list for the kids, as well as some snacks, seltzer, and coffee.

That's it. In fewer than 20 minutes, Carol is all set for a week of easy, stress-free meals.

Bonus Recipes

Although I tested the recipes in this book extensively to make them family-friendly, it's impossible to create 4 weeks of meal plans that will work for absolutely everyone. That's why I included 9 bonus recipes—3 for each meal—that you can easily swap for a meal you don't like.

Grocery Shopping Tips

As someone with two small children and limited time, I understand your pain when it comes to the grocery store. You likely are thinking, "It takes up so much time," "I always spend so much money and then get home and feel like I have nothing," or, "Half the time I don't even know what I am buying."

That's all about to change. When you're armed with a meal plan, shopping list, and some easy strategies, grocery shopping can be easy, affordable, and, dare I say, enjoyable.

Shop Once

The more often I go to the grocery store, the more I spend. Inevitably, I end up buying things I don't need. Not to mention all the extra time it takes to make an extra list, shop, and put away the groceries.

With that said, there are real concerns about safely storing food for a full week. We will get into specifics starting on page 22, but generally speaking, I freeze any meat I will not be using within 3 days. Then I let it defrost in the fridge the night before I need it.

In terms of produce, things can get a little tricky. Generally speaking, if I buy produce that is extremely fresh and store it properly, I find it lasts all week. For the few items that don't, I will make a quick weekday trip to the store to purchase produce only.

Take Inventory

Before I walk out the door to shop, I always do a quick inventory check in the pantry, fridge, and freezer. More often than not, I will find that I already have the things I thought I needed.

I also keep my eyes open for easy swaps during this time. Perhaps a recipe calls for black beans, but I have some pinto beans I could easily use. Maybe I can use frozen veggies in place of fresh. I am always looking for ways to use up what I already have.

Looking to save money? This is a good time to compare your list to local store circulars. Look for ingredients that are on sale or search for places you can make easy substitutions, like using blueberries instead of strawberries or ground turkey instead of ground chicken.

Stick to the List

The thing people are most afraid of when it comes to eating healthfully and meal planning is the cost. However, if you stick to your list, you will save money and waste less.

Another small tip that helps you stick to your list is this: Don't go to the store hungry, and leave your kids and spouse at home if possible. I can't tell you how much extra stuff I buy when I am hungry or have family members in tow.

Buy in Bulk

Buying in bulk is a proven way to save money, whether it be from bulk bins, sales, or warehouse stores. However, make sure you only buy things in bulk that you will actually use.

Splurge and Save

When I grocery shop, I tend to place items into two categories: items that will help me save money and items that are worth the splurge. For example, when it comes to staples like canned beans, pasta, oats, or frozen veggies, I always reach for the store brand. However, when it comes to an ingredient where the flavor really matters, like specialty cheese or spaghetti sauce, I reach for my favorite brands that I know taste amazing.

Another consideration here is buying organic. Generally speaking, buying organic is a healthier option since you can be sure your food is free from pesticides, genetically modified ingredients, antibiotics, and more. However, organic food can be more expensive.

In our home, I try to buy organic ingredients as often as I can and always stock up when I see organic products on sale, especially premium products like meat and poultry.

Food Storage and Safety

One of the most common questions I get when it comes to grocery shopping and meal prep is about safe food storage. How long can you keep things in the fridge, and what is the best way to store them?

Containers

Generally speaking, I recommend stocking your kitchen with an array of glass storage containers and Mason jars before starting your meal planning program.

There are many reasons that I prefer glass compared to plastic storage containers:

- **Glass is safe:** With glass storage containers, you don't have to worry about any chemicals or toxins leaching into your food. This happens most often when hot foods are stored in plastic or when food is heated up in plastic containers. To be on the safe side, I always choose glass when possible.

- **Glass can go from the freezer to the fridge.** Glass containers are more multifunctional and transfer from the fridge to freezer and vice versa without problems. You also don't have to worry about changing containers when reheating food, since glass doesn't melt or warp. Some glass can even transfer from the fridge to the oven.

- **Glass is heatproof.** Glass containers conduct and store heat more evenly than plastic. This means you don't have to worry about the glass melting, warping, or producing hot spots during cooking or reheating.

- **Glass is easier to clean.** Glass containers don't soak up the smells, colors, or oils of what's inside. You don't have to worry that your container will be stained or ruined based on what you store in it.

- **Glass is better for the environment.** Reusable glass containers are better for the environment than plastic and are easier to recycle.

Food Storage Best Practices

Before we get into specifics regarding the different foods detailed in the following sections, let's start with the basics of safe food storage:

- **Always let food cool before refrigerating or freezing it.** For the best results, especially when freezing, let your food fully cool before storing it. We have all put something in the fridge too soon and have seen condensation on the container. This condensation is moisture that is escaping from the food. It can result in dry leftovers and freezer burn. With that said, most food needs to be refrigerated within 2 hours of being prepared, at the most. Once it cools, get it right into the fridge or freezer.

- **Use airtight containers.** Another critical component of proper food storage is using airtight containers. This helps keep the food fresh and free of outside contaminants and bacteria. When possible, try to use containers that fit the leftovers and leave little extra space. Also, when using storage bags, be sure to press out any extra air.

- **Label, label, label.** Although it may seem unnecessary, always label your containers. It will save you when you can't remember what day you cooked something. We use masking tape and markers in our house and every afternoon I do a quick check to see if anything needs to be placed in the freezer or eaten.

In the sections that follow, you will find recommendations for how to store common ingredients and meals as well as recommendations for how long you can safely store them in the fridge or freezer.

Poultry, Meat, and Seafood

- **Raw:** For fresh meats, it is best to follow the expiration date on the packaging since you don't know exactly when it was packed. Frozen meat can be stored for up to 4 months, according to the USDA. Once it is defrosted, use it within 1 to 2 days.

- **Cooked:** Cooked meats can be safely stored in the fridge for 3 to 4 days. If you freeze cooked meat, it should be used within 3 months of freezing, according to the USDA. Once it is defrosted, it should be consumed within 1 to 2 days.

Fresh Produce and Salads

- **Storing produce in the refrigerator:** Generally speaking, produce is best used within 5 to 7 days of purchase, but this can vary depending on the type of fruit or vegetable and how fresh it was when you purchased it. Many people, me included, find that most veggies will last at least one week when refrigerated and stored properly.

- **Storing produce in the freezer:** Vegetables usually do not hold up well in the freezer. Some fruit—like berries, bananas, peaches, and plums—can be frozen for later use.

- **Storing salads:** Salads are best stored with the dressing packed on the side.

Soups and Stews

- **Storing soups and stews in the refrigerator:** Soups and stews will generally stay fresh in an airtight container for 4 to 5 days in the fridge.

- **Storing soups and stews in the freezer:** Soups and stews can be frozen for up to 3 months.

Grains

- **Storing grains in the refrigerator:** Cooked rice, quinoa, couscous, farro, and other grains keep well in the fridge for 4 to 5 days when stored in an airtight container or bag.

- **Storing grains in the freezer:** Cooked grains will last 2 to 3 months in the freezer.

Prepared Meals

- **Storing prepared meals in the refrigerator:** Most prepared meals that contain meat, vegetables, and/or grains will stay fresh in the fridge for 3 to 4 days.

- **Storing prepared meals in the freezer:** If the meal is appropriate for freezing, it is best used within 2 to 3 months of freezing.

Meal Prep and Kitchen Hacks

Meal Prep

Spending a couple of hours on the weekend prepping for the week can significantly speed up weekday meal prep.

In each week's Game Plan (page 32, page 66, page 104, and page 142), I will include ideas for what can be prepped in advance.

Following are some things we normally prep in advance.

Grains

Grains such as white rice, brown rice, quinoa, millet, barley, farro, and so on are great options for meal prep. I normally prep my grains for the entire month, storing anything I need after the first week in the freezer.

Here is how I store my prepped grains:

- **Cooked:** Let the grains fully cool and then store them in the fridge for up to 5 days.

- **Frozen:** Let the grains fully cool and store them in freezer bags, laying them flat in the freezer for maximum storage. Reheat the grains in the microwave or on the stove with a touch of extra water or broth.

Dressings and Sauces

Make all of your salad dressings and sauces ahead of time. They will keep in the fridge for 1 to 2 weeks.

Spices

If you hate measuring spices during the week, make any spice rubs or mixes ahead of time and store them in a small container. Then just dump and go during the week.

Garlic

Garlic can't be minced or chopped in advance since it will actually get stronger as it sits and can change the flavor of the recipe. However, you can stop this process with the addition of some olive oil.

Start by peeling a few heads of garlic. Add them to a food processor and pulse until the garlic is minced. Add the garlic to a jar and cover the garlic with olive oil. Keep the jar in the fridge for 2 to 3 weeks. Another option is to freeze the minced garlic and oil in an ice cube tray to create individual portions.

Vegetables

Prep time quickly adds up when you are dicing and slicing multiple vegetables. Every week when I get home from the market, I spend some time prepping veggies for the week. This saves me 10 to 15 minutes every night. Following are some vegetables and how to prep them:

- **Asparagus:** Trim the ends, then wash and dry the spears. Store them in an herb keeper for 5 to 7 days.

- **Brussels sprouts:** Wash and dry the Brussels sprouts, then remove any browned leaves and halve, quarter, or shred the sprouts. Keep them in an airtight container with a damp paper towel for 5 to 7 days.

- **Broccoli:** Wash, dry, and cut the broccoli into florets. Store the florets in an airtight container for up to 7 days.

- **Butternut squash:** Peel the squash, remove the seeds, and chop the squash. Keep it in an airtight container with a damp paper towel for 5 to 7 days.

- **Cabbage:** Wash and dry the cabbage, removing any damaged outside leaves. Chop or shred it, then store it in an airtight container for 5 to 7 days.

- **Cauliflower:** Wash and dry the cauliflower, then cut it into florets. Store the florets in an airtight container for up to 7 days.

- **Carrots:** Wash and peel the carrots, then cut them as desired. Keep them in an airtight container with a damp paper towel for 5 to 7 days.

- **Celery:** Wash the celery, then cut it as desired. Place it in an airtight container and cover it with cold water. Store the celery for 7 to 10 days.

- **Cucumber:** Wash and dry the cucumber. Peel it if needed. Slice it into rounds. If you are slicing it into sticks or half-circles, scoop out the seeds. Keep the cucumber in an airtight container with a damp paper towel for 3 to 4 days.

- **Green beans:** Wash, dry, and trim the green beans. Chop them if needed. Store them in an airtight container for up to 7 days.

- **Lettuce:** Wash and dry the lettuce well. Chop it and store it in an airtight container for 5 to 7 days.

- **Onions:** Remove the onions' skins and cut them as needed. Keep onions in an airtight container with a damp paper towel for 3 to 4 days. (Note that this prep method may make your fridge smell like onion.)

- **Peppers (bell pepper or spicy peppers):** Wash and dry the peppers well. Chop them and store them in an airtight container for 3 to 4 days.

- **Summer squash and zucchini:** Wash and dry the summer squash and zucchini. Cut them as needed. Keep them in an airtight container with a damp paper towel for 4 to 6 days.

I don't recommend prepping most fresh herbs, mushrooms, raw potatoes, raw sweet potatoes, or tomatoes in advance.

Prepared Meals

There are lots of meals you can fully prep ahead of time, like pancakes, oatmeal, salads, meatballs, meatloaf, fried rice, casseroles, and other dishes. These meals are listed in each week's Game Plan.

Kitchen Hacks

The other way to save time in the kitchen is by strategically using store-bought products to speed up weekday meals. Usually these options are more expensive, so I tend to save them for nights when I am extra busy.

Each week, I will include ideas for kitchen hacks in the weekly Game Plan.

Grains

There are tons of options for both frozen and shelf-stable rice, quinoa, barley, and other grains in the grocery store. If you use these often, consider making your own or buying them at a warehouse store.

Pasta

If even boiling pasta feels like too much, there are now parboiled pasta options that can be cooked in fewer than 2 minutes in the microwave. You can also parboil your own pasta and reheat it in boiling water.

Vegetables

Depending on the vegetable and recipe, you can sometimes swap frozen or canned vegetables for fresh. This cuts down on prep and cooking time. If chopping time is what you are worried about, look for precut veggies in the produce section or raid the salad bar. You can also buy bagged fresh produce that is already prepped (like broccoli florets, cauliflower florets, trimmed green beans, and more).

Proteins

For some recipes, you may be able to substitute precooked proteins like rotisserie chicken, meatballs, or precooked sausages to replace a raw protein. You can also consider using a protein that cooks more quickly, like shrimp, or simply cutting something like chicken into smaller pieces that will cook more rapidly.

Sauces, Salsas, Dressings, and Spices

Many times, it might make sense to grab something premade rather than make your own. It saves time measuring, mixing, and prepping. Plus, depending on how well stocked your pantry is, it might be more cost-effective. Just be aware that many times these options are less healthy than homemade items.

Garlic and Ginger

If you hate spending time mincing garlic and ginger, consider buying the refrigerated tubes. They keep in the fridge for 2 to 3 months and are huge time-savers.

Week 1

Woo-hoo! It's time to start your new life! Just kidding. Seriously, though, I couldn't be more excited for you to begin. Meal planning will make mealtime healthier, easier, and more joyful. As you start this process, remember that it takes time to learn a new skill and this is no different. Although most of the hard work is done for you, you will still want to dedicate some time to tailoring this plan to your needs.

Weekly Calendar

	Breakfast	Lunch	Dinner
Sunday	Zucchini Banana Bread Baked Oatmeal (A, page 35) *with ½ cup (125 g) Greek yogurt*	Barbecue Chicken "Empanadas" (D, page 40) *with 1 cup (30 g) greens*	Slow Cooker Mediterranean Beef with Tzatziki (E, page 43) *with Israeli Salad (F, page 44) and whole-wheat pita bread*
Monday	Turkey Bacon and Spinach Breakfast Sandwiches (B, page 36) *with fresh fruit*	Slow Cooker Mediterranean Beef with Tzatziki* (E, page 43) *with whole-wheat pita and ½ cup (15 g) greens*	One-Pot Creamy Sausage and Pepper Pasta (G, page 47)
Tuesday	Zucchini Banana Bread Baked Oatmeal* (A, page 35) *with ½ cup (125 g) Greek yogurt*	Barbecue Chicken "Empanadas"* (D, page 40) *with 1 cup (30 g) greens*	Cashew Chicken and Pineapple Fried Rice (H, page 48) *with edamame in pods*
Wednesday	Turkey Bacon and Spinach Breakfast Sandwiches* (B, page 36) *with fresh fruit*	Slow Cooker Mediterranean Beef with Tzatziki* (E, page 43) *with whole-wheat pita and ½ cup (15 g) greens*	Baked Pizza Pork Chops with Cauliflower (I, page 51) *with Crispy Herb Polenta Fries (J, page 52)*
Thursday	Zucchini Banana Bread Baked Oatmeal* (A, page 35) *with ½ cup (125 g) Greek yogurt*	Cashew Chicken and Pineapple Fried Rice* (H, page 48)	Skillet Turkey Enchiladas (K, page 55)
Friday	Turkey Bacon and Spinach Breakfast Sandwiches* (B, page 36) *with fresh fruit*	Skillet Turkey Enchiladas* (K, page 55)	One-Pan Honey Mustard Salmon, Potatoes, and Broccoli (L, page 56)
Saturday	Blueberry-Banana Greek Yogurt Pancakes (C, page 39)	One-Pan Honey Mustard Salmon, Potatoes, and Broccoli* (L, page 56) *over 1 cup (30 g) greens*	Cheddar-Apple Chicken Burgers (M, page 59) *with whole-wheat buns and Potato Zucchini Muffin Tots (N, page 60)*

* Indicates leftovers

Shopping List

Dairy and Refrigerated Items

- 2 cups (480 ml) unsweetened almond milk (A, C)
- 14 eggs (A, B, C, D, H, N)
- 3 cups (750 g) flavored Greek yogurt (A)
- ¼ cup (60 ml) skim milk (B)
- 6 slices Swiss cheese (B)
- 1⅓ cups (332 g) plain Greek yogurt (C, E)
- 1½ cups (180 g) shredded Cheddar cheese (D, K, M, N)
- ⅛ cup (30 g) reduced-fat cream cheese (G)
- ⅛ cup (10 g) shredded Parmesan cheese (G)
- ⅓ cup (37 g) shredded part-skim mozzarella cheese (I)
- ¼ cup (58 g) reduced-fat sour cream (K)
- 1¼ cups (163 g) shredded hash brown potatoes (N)

Produce

- 3 bananas (A, C)
- 2 zucchini (A, N)
- 2 cups (60 g) baby spinach (B)
- Fresh fruit for breakfast (B)
- ½ cup (50 g) blueberries (C)
- 2 tbsp (6 g) cilantro (D)
- 5 tbsp (45 g) red onion (D, F)
- 8 cups (240 g) greens for salads (D, E, L)
- 13 cloves garlic (E, G, H, K, L)
- 2 onions (E, G, K)
- 3 Persian cucumbers (E, F)
- 3 lemons (E, F, L)
- 1 cup (150 g) cherry tomatoes (F)
- ¼ cup (15 g) parsley (F)
- ⅛ cup (8 g) fresh basil (G)
- 1 red bell pepper (G, H)
- 1 green bell pepper (G, K)
- 3 green onions (H, N)
- 1 tsp ginger (H)
- 1½ cups (248 g) coarsely chopped pineapple (H)
- 2 cups (460 g) cauliflower florets (I)
- 2 red potatoes (L)
- 3 cups (525 g) broccoli florets (L)
- ½ apple (M)

Meat, Poultry, and Fish

- 4 pieces turkey bacon (B)
- 1 rotisserie chicken (D, H)
- 2 lb (900 g) beef chuck roast (E)
- 8 oz (224 g) raw Italian chicken sausage (G)
- 10 oz (280 g) lean boneless pork chops (I)
- 2 tbsp (20 g) turkey pepperoni (I)
- 1 lb (450 g) 93% lean ground turkey (K)
- 1½ lb (675 g) salmon (L)
- 8 oz (224 g) ground chicken (M)

Grains, Pasta, and Bulk Items

- 2⅓ cups (187 g) old-fashioned oats (A, C)
- 1 tbsp (10 g) chia seeds (A)
- ¾ cup (98 g) white whole-wheat flour (C)
- 2 cups (320 g) cooked brown rice (H)

Packaged, Canned, and Jarred Items

- ¼ cup (45 g) peanut butter (A)
- 6 English muffins (B)
- 4 flour tortillas (D)
- ½ cup (120 ml) low-sugar barbecue sauce (D)
- ¼ cup (63 g) canned corn (D)
- 6 whole-wheat pitas (E)
- 4 oz (112 g) penne (G)
- 1⅔ cups (400 ml) chicken broth (G)
- ¾ cup (169 g) canned fire-roasted diced tomatoes (G)
- 1 cup (150 g) frozen peas and carrots (H)
- 2 cups (236 g) frozen edamame in pods (H)

(Continued)

Shopping List (Continued)

- 1¼ cups (280 g) spaghetti sauce (I, J)
- 1 (12-oz [336-g]) tube polenta (J)
- 15 oz (420 g) canned pinto beans (K)
- 2 cups (480 ml) salsa verde (K)
- 6 corn tortillas (K)
- 2 whole-wheat burger buns (M)

Pantry Spices
- Pure vanilla extract (A, C)
- Ground cinnamon (A, C)
- Ground coriander (E)
- Allspice (E)

- Dried dill (E, F)
- Dried oregano (E, K)
- Ground cumin (E, K)
- Paprika (F)
- Italian seasoning (I, J, L)
- Garlic powder (I, J, L, M, N)
- Poultry seasoning (M)
- Kosher salt

Refrigerated Items
- Asian garlic chili paste (H)
- Low-sodium soy sauce (H)
- Butter (L)
- Dijon mustard (L)

Other Items
- ⅓ cup (60 g) chocolate chips (A)
- 3 tbsp (45 ml) pure maple syrup (A, C)
- Baking powder (A, C)
- Olive oil (B, E, F, L, M, N)
- Baking soda (C)
- ⅓ cup (37 g) raw cashews (H)
- Coconut oil (H)
- Honey (L)
- Burger toppings (M)
- Cooking spray

Game Plan

It's week one! Let's get organized so you are ready to attack the week ahead. Remember, the following tips are optional but will help make things easier during the week.

Meal Prep
- Prep the rotisserie chicken by removing the skin and chopping the meat. Set aside 1⅓ cups (186 g) for the Barbecue Chicken "Empanadas" (D, page 40) and 1½ cups (210 g) for the Cashew Chicken and Pineapple Fried Rice (H, page 48).

- Make the Turkey Bacon and Spinach Breakfast Sandwiches (B, page 36). Store them in the fridge or freezer.

- Cook the brown rice for the Cashew Chicken and Pineapple Fried Rice (H, page 48). Alternatively, cook this entire dish and simply reheat it on Tuesday.

- Make the Blueberry-Banana Greek Yogurt Pancakes (C, page 39) and freeze them.

- Prep the produce like so:

  - **Onions:** 1½ onions, diced (E, page 43; K, page 55); ½ onion, thinly sliced (G, page 47)

  - **Red onions:** 5 tbsp (45 g), diced (D, page 40; F, page 44)

  - **Red bell peppers:** ½ pepper, thinly sliced (G, page 47); ½ pepper, diced (H, page 48)

  - **Green bell pepper:** ½ pepper, thinly sliced (G, page 47); ½ pepper, diced (K, page 55)

  - **Pineapple:** 1½ cups (248 g), coarsely chopped (H, page 48)

  - **Cauliflower:** 2 cups (460 g) florets (I, page 51)

  - **Broccoli:** 3 cups (525 g) florets (L, page 56)

  - Prep fruit for breakfasts

  - Measure out greens for lunches

- Freeze the ground turkey, salmon, and ground chicken if needed.

Daily Tips

- **Sunday:** Start the Slow Cooker Mediterranean Beef with Tzatziki (E, page 43). Start the beef in the morning (it takes 8 hours) and make the tzatziki ahead so it has time to set in the fridge.

- **Tuesday:** Simply follow the instructions on the package for the edamame. Season it with salt or soy sauce.

- **Wednesday:** Start the Crispy Herb Polenta Fries (J, page 52) and the cauliflower in the oven at the same time. Place the ground turkey in the fridge to defrost overnight for Thursday's dinner.

- **Thursday:** Place the salmon in the fridge to defrost overnight for Friday's dinner.

- **Friday:** Place the ground chicken in the fridge to defrost overnight for Saturday's dinner.

- **Saturday:** Start with the Potato Zucchini Muffin Tots (N, page 60), since they take longer than the burger. You can prep the burgers from start to finish while the tots cook.

Kitchen Hacks

- **Sunday:** Buy store-bought tzatziki instead of making your own for dinner.

- **Monday:** Save some time on dinner by using precooked sausage instead of raw. Add it at the same time as the pasta so it doesn't overcook. You may need to up the spices and seasoning since the raw sausage adds flavor to the whole dish.

- **Tuesday:** Use frozen or precooked shelf-stable brown rice instead of prepping your own for dinner.

- **Saturday:** If the tots seem like too much work, buy frozen veggie tots instead. Or serve dinner with some raw carrots and celery sticks.

Zucchini Banana Bread Baked Oatmeal (A)

There is nothing better than serving up a wholesome breakfast packed with fruit, veggies, whole grains, and healthy fats that your family mistakes for dessert. My kids go crazy for this recipe, and it also doubles as a healthy after-school snack.

Serves: 6

Total Time: 45 minutes

2 very ripe bananas

1½ cups (360 ml) unsweetened almond milk

¼ cup (45 g) peanut butter

2 tbsp (30 ml) maple syrup

1 egg

1 tsp pure vanilla extract

2 cups (160 g) old-fashioned oats

1 tbsp (10 g) chia seeds

1 tsp ground cinnamon

½ tsp baking powder

¼ tsp salt

1 zucchini, finely shredded and gently squeezed of excess moisture

⅓ cup (60 g) chocolate chips (optional)

Preheat the oven to 350°F (177°C). Spray an 8 x 8-inch (20 x 20-cm) baking dish with cooking spray.

In a large bowl, mash the bananas with a fork. Add the almond milk, peanut butter, maple syrup, egg, and vanilla. Whisk until the ingredients are well combined and there are no large chunks of peanut butter.

Add the oats, chia seeds, cinnamon, baking powder, and salt. Stir to combine the ingredients. Fold in the zucchini and chocolate chips (if using).

Bake the oatmeal for 35 to 40 minutes, until the oatmeal is set and the top is golden brown. Let the oatmeal cool for at least 10 minutes before serving.

Picky Eaters: *Have a kid who refuses to eat anything green? Try peeling your zucchini before shredding it. It will blend right into the oats and no one will realize they are eating veggies for breakfast. The chocolate chips also serve as a great distraction.*

Turkey Bacon and Spinach Breakfast Sandwiches (B)

Ditch the drive-through and make your own amazing breakfast sandwiches at home. They keep in the freezer for up to 3 months, making them a staple in any busy home for a quick, filling on-the-go breakfast.

Serves: 6

Total Time: 40 minutes

4 pieces turkey bacon, finely chopped

2 cups (60 g) baby spinach, finely chopped

8 eggs

¼ cup (60 ml) skim milk

½ tsp kosher salt

¼ tsp black pepper

6 white or whole-wheat English muffins

1 tbsp (15 ml) olive oil

6 slices Swiss cheese

Preheat the oven to 350°F (177°C). Spray an 8 x 8–inch (20 x 20–cm) baking dish with cooking spray.

Heat a medium skillet over medium-high heat. Add the bacon and cook for 4 to 5 minutes, until it is crispy. Add the spinach and cook for 1 to 2 minutes, until it is wilted. Remove the skillet from the heat and set it aside to cool.

In a medium bowl, whisk together the eggs, milk, salt, and black pepper. Scatter the bacon and spinach mixture in the baking dish. Pour the eggs over the top of the bacon and spinach mixture.

Bake the eggs for 22 to 25 minutes, until they are just fluffy and set. Do not turn off the oven. Let the eggs cool completely, about 15 minutes. Cut the eggs into 6 pieces.

Increase the oven's temperature to broil. Place the English muffin halves on a small baking sheet and brush them with the oil. Broil the English muffins for 2 to 4 minutes, just until they have browned. Remove the English muffins from the oven and let them cool.

Layer one piece of egg and one slice of Swiss cheese on one half of the English muffins. Top the sandwiches with the other muffin halves. Wrap the sandwiches in plastic wrap or foil. Before serving, add something fresh to your sandwich, like tomato, avocado, salsa, greens, or a splash of hot sauce.

Storage and Reheating: *Keep these sandwiches in the fridge for up to 5 days or in the freezer for up to 3 months. To reheat them from the fridge, microwave the sandwiches for 1 to 1½ minutes. Alternatively, wrap the sandwiches in foil and reheat them in an oven preheated to 400°F (204°C) for 8 to 10 minutes. To reheat them from frozen, microwave the sandwiches for 2½ to 3 minutes wrapped in a moist paper towel. Alternatively, wrap the sandwiches in foil and reheat them in an oven preheated to 400°F (204°C) for 10 to 15 minutes.*

Make It Yours: *Think of this recipe as a blueprint to make all your favorites using any combination of eggs, cooked veggies, meat, and cheese you like. Classic combos include broccoli and Cheddar, diced ham and bell peppers, turkey sausage and kale, or black beans and salsa.*

Blueberry-Banana Greek Yogurt Pancakes (C)

These protein-packed pancakes are one of the most requested weekend breakfasts in our home. Unlike traditional pancakes that leave you starving after an hour, these pancakes are packed with protein and fiber to keep you energized all morning. Plus, the bananas add natural sweetness so you won't need a river of maple syrup.

Serves: 2

Total Time: 20 minutes

¾ cup (98 g) white whole-wheat flour

⅓ cup (27 g) old-fashioned oats

½ tsp baking powder

¼ tsp baking soda

¼ tsp ground cinnamon

Pinch of salt

½ to ¾ cup (120 to 180 ml) unsweetened almond milk

⅓ cup (83 g) plain or flavored Greek yogurt

1 ripe banana, mashed

1 egg

1 tbsp (15 ml) maple syrup

¼ tsp pure vanilla extract

½ cup (50 g) fresh or frozen blueberries

Oil of choice, as needed

In a large bowl, combine the flour, oats, baking powder, baking soda, cinnamon, and salt. In a medium bowl, combine the milk, yogurt, banana, egg, maple syrup, and vanilla. Add the milk mixture to the flour mixture. Stir until the two are just combined. Do not overmix the batter, since this makes the pancakes dense. Fold in the blueberries.

Heat a griddle over medium-high heat. Add the oil. Add ¼ cup (60 ml) of batter for each pancake. Cook the pancakes for 3 to 4 minutes, until the tops are bubbling. Flip the pancakes and cook for 2 to 3 minutes, until they are cooked through.

If needed, keep the cooked pancakes warm in an oven preheated to 250°F (121°C). Top the pancakes with pure maple syrup, nut butter, honey, fresh fruit, or yogurt.

Leftover Love: *Pancakes are a staple in my freezer. To freeze these pancakes, let them cool completely. Then place them on a baking sheet and freeze them for 2 to 3 hours, until the outsides are frozen. Place the pancakes in a freezer bag or freezer-safe container. Store them in the freezer for up to 3 months. Reheat the pancakes in the microwave or in a skillet.*

Barbecue Chicken "Empanadas" (D)

I didn't know what to call this recipe. Are these empanadas, quesadillas, or calzones? No matter what you call them, these crispy and cheesy barbecue chicken pockets will be your new favorite lunch.

Serves: 4

Total Time: 25 minutes

1⅓ cups (186 g) cooked finely chopped chicken

½ cup (120 ml) low-sugar barbecue sauce

½ cup (60 g) shredded Cheddar cheese

¼ cup (63 g) canned corn

2 tbsp (6 g) finely chopped fresh cilantro

2 tbsp (18 g) diced red onion

4 flour tortillas

1 egg, beaten

Preheat the oven to 400°F (204°C). Spray a medium baking sheet with cooking spray.

In a medium bowl, toss together the chicken, barbecue sauce, Cheddar cheese, corn, cilantro, and red onion. Distribute the filling evenly among the tortillas, arranging the filling on one half of the tortillas. Fold over the tortillas and use a fork to press down on the edges and seal the "empanadas."

Brush the empanadas with the egg. Bake the empanadas for 12 to 14 minutes, until they are crispy and brown. Let the empanadas cool for 2 minutes before cutting them.

Recipe Blueprint: *Stuff your empanadas with all of your favorite fillings. Take inspiration from pizza with marinara sauce, mozzarella cheese, and mushrooms. Go Mexican with chicken, enchilada sauce, and beans. Or just grab your favorite cooked veggies, cheese, and pesto for a savory treat.*

Slow Cooker Mediterranean Beef with Tzatziki (E)

We are lucky enough to live near lots of amazing Mediterranean restaurants. But restaurant food quickly gets expensive, so instead of ordering in, I love to make this Mediterranean-inspired beef with a quick homemade tzatziki. We use the sauce for sandwiches, grain bowls, salads, and more.

Serves: 6

Total Time: 8 hours, 15 minutes

Beef

2 lb (900 g) beef chuck roast, trimmed

1 tbsp (15 ml) olive oil

1½ tbsp (5 g) dried oregano

1½ tsp (9 g) kosher salt

1 tsp ground cumin

½ tsp ground coriander

½ tsp black pepper

¼ tsp allspice

1 onion, diced

4 cloves garlic, minced

Tzatziki

1 Persian cucumber

1 cup (250 g) 2% or whole-milk plain Greek yogurt

½ tsp grated garlic

1 tbsp (15 ml) fresh lemon juice

1 tsp lemon zest

1 tsp olive oil

¼ tsp dried dill

¼ tsp black pepper

Salt, as needed

To make the beef, cut the beef chuck roast into 1-inch (2.5-cm) pieces, trimming the fat as needed. Add the oil to a large, heavy skillet over medium-high heat. Add the beef and sear it for 3 to 4 minutes, until it is brown. Flip the beef and cook it for 3 to 4 minutes, until it is brown. Transfer the beef to a large slow cooker. You can skip this step, but it adds flavor and color. If you choose to skip this step, omit the oil from the recipe.

In a small bowl, mix together the oregano, salt, cumin, coriander, black pepper, and allspice. Sprinkle this mixture over the beef in the slow cooker and stir to coat the beef. Stir in the onion and garlic. Cook the beef on low for 8 hours.

To make the tzatziki, finely grate the cucumber. Use a paper towel or kitchen towel to squeeze out as much of the cucumber's moisture as possible. Transfer the cucumber to a medium bowl. Add the yogurt, garlic, lemon juice, lemon zest, oil, dill, black pepper, and salt to taste. Stir to combine the ingredients. Place the tzatziki in the fridge to chill for at least 2 hours before serving.

Serve the beef drizzled with the tzatziki in a pita, over rice, or on a bed of greens.

Picky Eaters: *Instead of serving this as a sandwich with the beef, tzatziki, and Israeli Salad (page 44), make your kids an appetizer plate. Toast some pita wedges to make "chips" and serve them alongside the beef, cucumber slices, cherry tomatoes, and tzatziki for dipping.*

Israeli Salad (F)

When I first met my husband, this was pretty much the only salad he would eat. I am proud to say that has since changed, but we both still love this classic salad packed with crunchy veggies and bright flavors.

Serves: 2

Total Time: 10 minutes

2 Persian cucumbers, finely chopped

1 cup (150 g) cherry tomatoes, finely chopped

¼ cup (15 g) fresh parsley, finely chopped

3 tbsp (27 g) diced red onion

1½ tbsp (23 ml) fresh lemon juice

1 tbsp (15 ml) olive oil

½ tsp dried dill

¼ tsp paprika

Salt, as needed

Black pepper, as needed

In a medium bowl, combine the cucumbers, tomatoes, parsley, and onion.

In a small bowl, stir together the lemon juice, oil, dill, and paprika to create the dressing.

Drizzle the dressing over the vegetables and stir to coat.

Season the salad with the salt and black pepper as needed.

Recipe Ideas: *There are so many ways to switch up the flavors in this classic salad. Stir in some Greek yogurt for a creamy version. Add chickpeas to make it heartier. Add a chopped jalapeño for some spice. Throw in some olives, capers, or pepperoncini for some zing. Try topping the whole salad with some crumbled feta cheese.*

One-Pot Creamy Sausage and Pepper Pasta (G)

This is a clear example of a healthyish recipe. It is significantly lightened up compared to a traditional creamy sausage pasta dish, using lean sausage, lots of veggies, and a lightened up tomato cream sauce.

Serves: 2

Total Time: 30 minutes

8 oz (224 g) raw sweet or spicy Italian chicken or turkey sausage

½ onion, thinly sliced

½ red bell pepper, thinly sliced

½ green bell pepper, thinly sliced

1 to 2 cloves garlic, minced

4 oz (112 g) penne pasta

1⅔ cups (400 ml) chicken broth

¾ cup (180 ml) canned fire-roasted diced tomatoes, undrained

⅛ cup (30 g) reduced-fat cream cheese

Salt, as needed

Black pepper, as needed

⅛ cup (10 g) Parmesan cheese

⅛ cup (8 g) fresh basil leaves, torn

Heat a large pot over medium-high heat.

Use the tip of a knife to slice through the sausage casing lengthwise. Remove the casing and add the sausage to the pot. Brown the sausage for 4 to 6 minutes, breaking it up as it cooks. Add the onion, red bell pepper, green bell pepper, and garlic. Cook the mixture for 4 to 5 minutes, until the vegetables have softened.

Stir in the penne, broth, and diced tomatoes. Bring the mixture to a boil, then reduce the heat to medium-low. Stir the pasta and cover the pot. Cook the pasta for 12 to 15 minutes, stirring halfway through the cooking time, until the pasta is al dente and most of the liquid has been absorbed. Stir in the cream cheese. Cook the pasta for 2 to 3 minutes. Turn off the heat and let the pasta sit for 2 to 3 minutes to allow the sauce to thicken. Season the pasta with the salt and black pepper. Top it with the Parmesan cheese and basil.

Kitchen Tip: *If you have never made a one-pot pasta dish, you may get scared the pasta won't cook, especially as it absorbs the liquid. Trust the process and avoid the temptation to add more liquid. By the time the pasta is done, you want almost all the liquid to be absorbed by the pasta.*

Cashew Chicken and Pineapple Fried Rice (H)

When you are tempted to pick up the phone and order takeout, think about making this amazing fried rice instead. Your kids will go crazy for the sweetness of the pineapple and you will feel good knowing they are eating a meal packed with veggies, fruit, whole grains, and lean protein. And the leftovers? Delicious.

Serves: 4

Total Time: 25 minutes

2 tbsp (30 g) coconut oil or 2 tbsp (30 ml) vegetable oil, divided

2 eggs, beaten

2 green onions, minced

2 cloves garlic, minced

1 tbsp (15 ml) Asian garlic chili paste (optional)

1 tsp minced fresh ginger

1½ cups (248 g) coarsely chopped pineapple

½ red bell pepper, diced

1 cup (150 g) frozen peas and carrots

2 cups (320 g) cooked and cooled brown rice

1½ cups (210 g) coarsely chopped cooked boneless, skinless chicken

⅓ cup (37 g) raw cashews

3 tbsp (45 ml) low-sodium soy sauce, plus more as needed

Heat 1 tablespoon (15 g) of the oil in a large skillet over high heat. Add the eggs. Scramble the eggs for 1 to 2 minutes, until they are just cooked through. Remove the eggs from the skillet and set them aside.

Add the remaining 1 tablespoon (15 g) of oil to the skillet. Add the green onions, garlic, Asian garlic chili paste (if using), and ginger. Cook the mixture for 30 seconds. Add the pineapple, bell pepper, and peas and carrots. Cook the mixture for 3 to 4 minutes, until the pineapple begins to caramelize. Add the rice, chicken, and cashews. Stir to combine the ingredients.

Press the rice into the bottom of the skillet with the back of a spoon. Cook the rice for 2 to 3 minutes, until it begins to turn brown and crispy. Repeat this step if desired for more crispy rice.

Stir in the scrambled eggs and soy sauce. Taste and add more soy sauce as needed.

Kitchen Hack: *Don't have time to prep the rice or chicken? Let the grocery store do the heavy lifting. Grab some frozen brown rice and cook it for two-thirds of the suggested cooking time. Then grab a rotisserie chicken or some cooked chicken breast. You can even grab the green onions, red bell pepper, and pineapple from the salad bar.*

Baked Pizza Pork Chops with Cauliflower (I)

One of my favorite ways to get my kids to eat an unfamiliar food is to turn it into pizza. Add some sauce and cheese, and I can get them to eat just about anything. We usually do this with veggies, although lately I have been trying it with proteins—it works like a charm.

Serves: 2

Total Time: 35 minutes

2 cups (460 g) cauliflower florets

1 tbsp (15 ml) olive oil, divided

1 tsp Italian seasoning, divided

Salt, as needed

Black pepper, as needed

2 (5-oz [140-g]) lean boneless pork chops

½ tsp garlic powder

⅔ cup (160 ml) spaghetti sauce

⅓ cup (37 g) shredded part-skim mozzarella cheese

2 tbsp (20 g) coarsely chopped turkey pepperoni

Preheat the oven to 400°F (204°C).

In a large glass baking dish, toss the cauliflower with ½ tablespoon (8 ml) of the oil, ½ teaspoon of the Italian seasoning, salt, and black pepper. Spread the cauliflower out in a single layer and roast it for 10 minutes, until it is beginning to brown and soften.

Meanwhile, brush the pork chops on both sides with the remaining ½ tablespoon (7 ml) of oil. Sprinkle them with the remaining ½ teaspoon of Italian seasoning, garlic powder, and salt.

Carefully remove the baking dish from the oven. Nestle the pork chops into the dish among the cauliflower. Cook the pork chops and cauliflower for 12 minutes.

Carefully remove the baking dish from the oven and cover the pork chops and cauliflower with the spaghetti sauce. Sprinkle the mozzarella cheese and pepperoni over top. Return the baking dish to the oven and cook for 8 to 10 minutes, until the pork's internal temperature reaches 145°F (63°C).

Know Your Ingredients: *There are so many different options for jarred pasta sauce, it can be hard to know what to choose. Always look for a sauce with little or, better yet, no added sugar. Make sure the ingredient list includes only things you recognize, and avoid sauces with high-fructose corn syrup and added preservatives.*

Crispy Herb Polenta Fries (J)

Crispy on the outside and tender on the inside, these easy polenta fries are a great new side dish to add to your repertoire. Store-bought polenta makes them easy, and kids love the familiar flavor of corn. In my family, they are known as cornbread fries, and I'm okay with that.

Serves: 2

Total Time: 35 minutes

1 (12-oz [336-g]) tube polenta

1 tbsp (15 ml) olive oil

1 tsp garlic powder

½ tsp Italian seasoning

Salt, as needed

Black pepper, as needed

½ cup (120 ml) spaghetti sauce

Preheat the oven to 400°F (204°C). Spray a large baking sheet with cooking spray.

Cut the polenta into slices that are about ¾ inch (2 cm) thick. Then cut those slices into fries that are about ¾ inch (2 cm) wide. Transfer the fries to the prepared baking sheet.

Gently toss the polenta fries with the oil, garlic powder, Italian seasoning, salt, and black pepper.

Spread out the polenta fries in a single layer, so that they aren't touching. Bake the polenta fries for 30 minutes, flipping them halfway through the cooking time, until they are brown and crispy. Serve the polenta fries with the spaghetti sauce for dipping.

Kitchen Tip: *Tubed polenta is one of my favorite pantry staples to grab when I need a quick side dish. Although fries are our family favorite, you can cut the polenta into cubes for croutons, rounds for an easy appetizer, or "soldiers" for dipping into soup.*

Skillet Turkey Enchiladas (K)

If there are enchiladas on a menu, you better bet that I am ordering them. But making them at home? That's another story. Even though they seem simple, they take forever. That's where this shortcut casserole comes in. All the same flavors without any of the rolling, stuffing, or fighting with broken tortillas.

Serves: 4

Total Time: 30 minutes

1 tsp olive oil

½ onion, diced

½ green bell pepper, poblano pepper, or jalapeño pepper, diced

2 cloves garlic, minced

1 lb (450 g) 93% lean ground turkey

1 tsp ground cumin

½ tsp dried oregano

¼ tsp salt, plus more as needed

15 oz (420 g) canned pinto beans, drained and rinsed

6 corn tortillas, cut in half and then into 1-inch (2.5-cm) strips

2 cups (480 ml) salsa verde

¼ cup (58 g) reduced-fat sour cream or cream cheese (optional)

½ cup (60 g) shredded Cheddar cheese

Heat the oil in a large skillet over medium-high heat. Add the onion and bell pepper. Cook the vegetables for 4 to 5 minutes, until they are tender. Add the garlic and cook it for 30 seconds, until it is fragrant. Add the turkey, cumin, oregano, and salt. Cook the mixture for 7 to 10 minutes, breaking up the turkey as it cooks, until the turkey is brown and cooked through. Taste the mixture and season it with additional salt if needed.

Stir in the pinto beans, tortillas, and salsa verde. Cook the mixture for 4 to 5 minutes, until it is heated through and the tortillas are soft. Stir in the sour cream, if using, until it is fully incorporated. Add the Cheddar cheese and cover. Cook the mixture for 2 to 3 minutes, until the cheese is melted.

Top the enchiladas with cilantro, avocado, jalapeños, diced tomatoes, or any other toppings you enjoy.

Reheating Tip: *If you are using the leftovers for lunch, add some extra salsa before reheating to keep everything moist and delicious.*

Know Your Ingredients: *In this recipe, I opt for salsa verde instead of standard enchilada sauce. Although enchilada sauce would work, I find the ingredients in salsa to be much cleaner—more veggies, fewer fillers and artificial flavors. And in case you're wondering, salsa definitely counts as a serving of veggies.*

One-Pan Honey Mustard Salmon, Potatoes, and Broccoli (L)

The honey mustard sauce in this recipe will have you licking your fingers for more. It's one of those simple sauces that will transform any protein, but I especially love it with the sweet flavors in salmon. Paired with crispy potatoes and broccoli, this salmon is a meal everyone will want again and again.

Serves: 4

Total Time: 40 minutes

2 red potatoes, cut into ½-inch (13-mm) pieces

2 tbsp (30 ml) olive oil, divided

1 tsp garlic powder

1 tsp kosher salt, divided

½ tsp black pepper, divided

1 tbsp (15 g) butter or 1 tbsp (15 ml) olive oil

1 to 2 cloves garlic, minced

3 tbsp (48 g) Dijon mustard or whole-grain mustard

3 tbsp (45 ml) honey

2 tbsp (30 ml) fresh lemon juice

1 tsp Italian seasoning

1½ lb (675 g) salmon

3 cups (525 g) broccoli florets

Preheat the oven to 400°F (204°C).

In a large bowl, toss the potatoes with 1 tablespoon (15 ml) of the oil, garlic powder, ½ teaspoon of the salt, and ¼ teaspoon of the black pepper. Spread the potatoes out in a single layer on a large baking sheet. Bake the potatoes for 15 to 20 minutes, until they are beginning to get crispy and tender.

Meanwhile, combine the butter, remaining olive oil, and garlic in a small bowl. Microwave the butter and garlic for 30 to 40 seconds, until the butter is melted and the garlic is fragrant. Stir in the mustard, honey, lemon juice, Italian seasoning, remaining ½ teaspoon of salt, and remaining ¼ teaspoon of black pepper.

Remove the baking sheet from the oven. Push the potatoes to one side. Add the salmon and broccoli. Pour the sauce over the salmon and toss the broccoli with any remaining sauce.

Return the baking sheet to the oven and cook the salmon and vegetables for 10 to 12 minutes, until the salmon is opaque and cooked through. If desired, increase the oven's temperature to broil for the last 2 minutes of cooking time for a crispier texture.

Recipe Ideas: *This recipe works with all kinds of different combinations of starches and veggies. Try sweet potatoes, baby fingerlings, or butternut squash and pair them with cauliflower, asparagus, green beans, or snap peas.*

Cheddar-Apple Chicken Burgers (M)

The secret to these burgers is the grated apple. It adds a subtle sweetness that kids love, but more importantly, it adds moisture to the burger, ensuring that it doesn't end up dry and flavorless. We usually eat these with barbecue sauce, sliced red onions, some extra apple slices, and arugula.

Serves: 2

Total Time: 15 minutes

8 oz (224 g) lean ground chicken

½ apple, peeled and grated

¼ cup (30 g) shredded Cheddar cheese

½ tsp poultry seasoning

¼ tsp garlic powder

¼ tsp kosher salt

⅛ tsp black pepper

½ tbsp (8 ml) olive oil

In a medium bowl, combine the chicken, apple, Cheddar cheese, poultry seasoning, garlic powder, salt, and black pepper. Gently combine the ingredients using your hands, and try not to compress the meat.

Divide the meat into portions and shape them into patties. Make a small indent in the center of each patty with your thumb to help it cook more evenly.

Heat the oil in a medium skillet over medium-high heat. Add the burgers and cook them for 4 to 5 minutes on each side, until the burgers' internal temperature reaches at least 165°F (74°C).

Picky Eaters: *For a long time, my kids didn't love the idea of burgers, so I would turn these into "nuggets" and just make some mini burgers to serve with their favorite dipping sauce. If needed, you could also dredge them in breadcrumbs to make them more familiar.*

Potato Zucchini Muffin Tots (N)

For years, I made my kids homemade veggie tots. They were a labor of love—molding them into the perfect little tot shape took forever. Then I discovered that I could re-create all the crispy texture and delicious taste in a mini muffin tin in half the time.

Serves: 2

Total Time: 15 minutes

1¼ cups (163 g) shredded hash brown potatoes

½ cup (75 g) shredded zucchini

1 green onion, finely chopped

¼ cup (30 g) shredded Cheddar cheese

1 egg white

½ tbsp (8 ml) olive oil

½ tbsp (4 g) white whole-wheat flour

½ tsp garlic powder

½ tsp kosher salt

¼ tsp black pepper

Preheat the oven 425°F (218°C). Liberally spray a mini muffin tin with cooking spray.

Using a paper towel or kitchen towel, squeeze any excess moisture out of the potatoes and zucchini. The more liquid you can get out of the vegetables (especially the zucchini), the crispier the tots will be.

In a medium bowl, mix together the potatoes, zucchini, green onion, Cheddar cheese, egg white, oil, flour, garlic powder, salt, and black pepper with your hands. If needed, add more flour to keep the mixture together.

Press about 1 rounded tablespoon (10 g) of the vegetable mixture into the wells of the mini muffin tin and spray the tops of the tots with cooking spray. Bake the tots for 20 to 25 minutes, until they are brown on the edges. Increase the oven's temperature to broil and cook the tots for 2 to 3 minutes to further brown on tops.

Leftover Love: *These tots freeze well, so I almost always make a double or triple batch. Just make sure to let them fully cool before placing them in a freezer-safe bag. Reheat them for 10 to 15 minutes in an oven preheated to 400°F (204°C).*

Week 2

Before we dive headfirst into week 2, let's take a moment to reflect. What worked really well during week 1? What was hard? What adjustments do you need to make as you head into this week? Maybe it's investing some extra time in meal prep. Perhaps you need to plan around an extra-busy night. Maybe you skipped a meal and want to include that in this week's plan. Whatever your circumstance, head into this week thinking about what will make the days ahead even more successful.

Weekly Calendar

	Breakfast	Lunch	Dinner
Sunday	Pepperoni Pizza Mini Frittatas (A, page 69) *with fresh fruit and whole-wheat toast*	Mason Jar Instant Lasagna Soup (D, page 74)	Slow Cooker Honey-Soy Chicken (E, page 77) *with Coconut Quinoa (F, page 78) and Spicy Asian Brussels Sprouts (G, page 81)*
Monday	Pumpkin–Chocolate Chip Muffins (B, page 70) *with ½ cup (125 g) yogurt*	Slow Cooker Honey-Soy Chicken* (E, page 77) *with Coconut Quinoa* (F, page 78) and ½ cup (59 g) shelled edamame*	Creamy Spinach and Artichoke Pasta (H, page 82)
Tuesday	Pepperoni Pizza Mini Frittatas* (A, page 69) *with fresh fruit and whole-wheat toast*	Mason Jar Instant Lasagna Soup* (D, page 74)	Broiled Barbecue Flank Steak with Mango Salsa (I, page 85) *with Cilantro-Lime Cauliflower Rice and Beans (J, page 86)*
Wednesday	Pumpkin–Chocolate Chip Muffins* (B, page 70) *with ½ cup (125 g) yogurt*	Slow Cooker Honey-Soy Chicken* (E, page 77) *with Cilantro-Lime Cauliflower Rice and Beans* (J, page 86)*	Skillet Pork Tenderloin with Apples and Snap Peas (K, page 89)
Thursday	Pepperoni Pizza Mini Frittatas* (A, page 69) *with fresh fruit and whole-wheat toast*	Broiled Barbecue Flank Steak with Mango Salsa* (I, page 85) *with 1 cup (30 g) greens*	Sheet-Pan Pesto Meatballs, Roasted Tomatoes, and Gnocchi (L, page 90)
Friday	Pumpkin–Chocolate Chip Muffins* (B, page 70) *with ½ cup (125 g) yogurt*	Skillet Pork Tenderloin with Apples and Snap Peas* (K, page 89)	Tomato-Basil Fish (M, page 93) *with Lemon-Garlic Roasted Broccoli and Polenta (N, page 94)*
Saturday	Ultimate Breakfast Scramble (C, page 73) *with fresh fruit and whole-wheat toast*	Sheet-Pan Pesto Meatballs, Roasted Tomatoes, and Gnocchi* (L, page 90)	Crispy Baked Sweet Potato Taquitos (O, page 97) *with Mexican Fruit Salad (P, page 98)*

* Indicates leftovers

Shopping List

Dairy and Refrigerated Items

- ¾ cup (180 ml) skim milk (A, B, C)
- 16 eggs (A, B, C, L)
- 1 cup (112 g) shredded part-skim mozzarella cheese (A, C, D)
- 3 cups (750 g) flavored Greek yogurt (B)
- 1 cup (130 g) shredded hash brown potatoes (C)
- ¼ cup (31 g) part-skim ricotta cheese (D)
- 2 tbsp (30 g) reduced-fat cream cheese (H)
- ⅔ cup (53 g) shredded Parmesan cheese (H, L, N)
- 2 tbsp (16 g) queso fresco cheese (P)

Produce

- Fresh fruit for breakfast (A, C)
- 5 cups (150 g) baby spinach (A, C, H)
- 1 carrot (B)
- 2 zucchini (D, L)
- ¼ cup (13 g) sliced green onions (E)
- 1 tbsp (3 g) minced ginger (E)
- 12 cloves garlic (E, H, J, M, O)
- 1 red onion (E, I, O)
- 8 oz (224 g) Brussels sprouts (G)
- ½ shallot (H)
- 1 mango (I)
- 2 cups (60 g) greens (I)
- 1 jalapeño (I)
- ¾ cup (36 g) cilantro (I, J, O, P)
- 3 limes (I, J, O, P)
- 2 cups (650 g) cauliflower rice (J)
- 2 apples (K)
- 2 cups (300 g) snap peas (K)
- 1 lb (450 g) Campari or Roma tomatoes (L)
- ⅓ cup (20 g) fresh basil (L, M)
- 2 cups (350 g) broccoli florets (N)
- ½ lemon (N)
- 1 cup (150 g) diced sweet potatoes (O)
- ½ avocado (O)
- 1 Persian cucumber (P)
- 1 cup (154 g) chopped watermelon (P)
- ½ cup (65 g) chopped jicama (P)

Meat, Poultry, and Fish

- 6 tbsp (54 g) turkey pepperoni (A)
- 4 precooked chicken sausages (C, D)
- 2 lb (900 g) boneless, skinless chicken thighs (E)
- 8 oz (224 g) boneless, skinless chicken breast (H)
- 1⅓ lb (600 g) lean flank steak (I)
- 1⅓ lb (600 g) lean pork tenderloin (K)
- 1 lb (450 g) lean ground chicken (L)
- 10 oz (280 g) white fish (like cod) (M)

Grains, Pasta, and Bulk Items

- Whole-wheat bread (A, C)
- 1 cup (80 g) old-fashioned oats (B)
- 4 cups (560 g) dry pasta (D, H)
- ⅔ cup (113 g) quinoa (F)
- 10 oz (280 g) potato gnocchi (L)

Packaged, Canned, and Jarred Items

- 2 cups (480 ml) spaghetti sauce (A, D)
- ½ cup (113 g) canned pumpkin puree (B)
- 2½ tbsp (35 g) tomato paste (D, L)
- 1 cup (118 g) shelled edamame (E)
- 1 cup (240 ml) canned coconut milk (F)
- 1 cup (168 g) artichoke hearts (H)
- 2 cups (480 ml) low-sodium chicken broth (H)
- 2¼ cups (135 g) canned black beans (J, O)
- 3 tbsp (48 g) pesto (L)
- 10 oz (280 g) canned San Marzano tomatoes (M)
- 1 (6-oz [168-g]) tube polenta (N)
- ⅔ cup (150 g) canned diced tomatoes with green chiles (O)
- 6 corn tortillas (O)
- ½ cup (120 ml) salsa verde (O)

(Continued)

Shopping List (Continued)

Pantry Spices

- Garlic powder (A, D, I, N)
- Onion powder (A, I, N)
- Dried oregano (A, J, M)
- Pure vanilla extract (B)
- Pumpkin pie spice (B)
- Ground cinnamon (B, K)
- Italian seasoning (D)
- Red pepper flakes (D)
- Grill seasoning (H, K)
- Paprika (I, O)

- Chili powder (I, O, P)
- Ground cumin (J, O)

Refrigerated Items

- Asian garlic chili paste (E, G)
- Low-sodium soy sauce (E, G)
- Butter (M)

Other Items

- Olive oil (A, H, I, K, M, N, O)
- ⅓ cup (60 g) chocolate chips (B)
- Pure maple syrup (B)
- Baking powder (B)
- 2 tbsp (18 g) chicken bouillon (D)

- Cornstarch (E)
- Rice vinegar (E, G)
- Honey (E, G, K, D)
- 2½ tbsp (13 g) unsweetened shredded coconut (F)
- Coconut oil (F)
- Brown sugar (F, I)
- Sesame oil (G)
- ¼ cup (14 g) whole-wheat panko breadcrumbs (L)
- Cooking spray

Game Plan

Most of this week's meals are quick and easy to prepare, but if you meal prep anything, make it the meatballs. Shredding the zucchini and rolling the meatballs is the most time-intensive step this week.

Meal Prep

- Make Pumpkin–Chocolate Chip Muffins (B, page 70). Store them in the fridge or freezer.

- Make Cilantro-Lime Cauliflower Rice and Beans (J, page 86).

- Make the meatballs for the Sheet-Pan Pesto Meatballs, Roasted Tomatoes, and Gnocchi (L, page 90). Keep them in the fridge or freezer. Defrost the night before if it is frozen.

- Make the filling for the Crispy Baked Sweet Potato Taquitos (O, page 97). Store it in the fridge or freezer.

- Prep the produce like so:

  - **Brussels sprouts:** 8 oz (224 g), halved (G, page 81)

  - **Jalapeño:** 1 pepper, diced (I, page 85)

  - **Red onion:** 1 onion, diced (I, page 85; O, page 97)

  - **Snap peas:** 2 cups (300 g), trimmed (K, page 89)

  - **Broccoli:** 2 cups (350 g) florets (N, page 94)

  - Prep fruit for breakfasts

  - Measure out edamame and greens for lunches

- Freeze the ground chicken and whitefish if needed.

Daily Tips

- **Sunday:** Start the Slow Cooker Honey-Soy Chicken (E, page 77) at least 4½ hours before dinner. Start the Coconut Quinoa (F, page 78), and then make the Spicy Asian Brussels Sprouts (G, page 81). The quinoa can stay warm covered on the stove while the Brussels sprouts finish.

- **Tuesday:** Make the Cilantro-Lime Cauliflower Rice and Beans (J, page 86) while the steak rests. Just make sure everything is prepped and ready before starting the steak.

- **Wednesday:** Place the ground chicken (or meatballs if you meal prepped) in the fridge to defrost overnight.

- **Thursday:** Place the fish in the fridge to defrost overnight.

- **Friday:** Start the Lemon-Garlic Roasted Broccoli and Polenta (N, page 94) before starting the fish. Add the fish to the baking sheet after you flip the broccoli and polenta.

- **Saturday:** Make the Mexican Fruit Salad (P, page 98) while the taquitos bake.

Kitchen Hacks

- **Sunday:** Make the sauce for the Slow Cooker Honey-Soy Chicken (E, page 77) on the stove and use a chopped rotisserie chicken. Use store-bought sweet chili sauce or teriyaki for the Spicy Asian Brussels Sprouts (G, page 81).

- **Monday:** Skip the raw chicken and add cooked rotisserie chicken to the pasta right before serving.

- **Tuesday:** Buy a ready-made fruit salsa instead of making the mango salsa. Use frozen or packaged cauliflower rice.

- **Thursday:** Replace the homemade meatballs with store-bought beef, turkey, or vegetarian meatballs.

- **Saturday:** Make soft tacos instead of taquitos. Grab a store-bought fruit salad and just make the dressing.

Pepperoni Pizza Mini Frittatas (A)

Mini frittatas are one of my go-to recipes for easy breakfasts and snacks. This pizza version is the one my kids request most often, and I am happy to oblige. Packed with protein and veggies, these portable bites are great for any meal.

Serves: 6

Total Time: 30 minutes

1 tsp olive oil

2 cups (60 g) baby spinach, finely chopped

9 eggs

½ cup (120 ml) spaghetti sauce

¼ cup (60 ml) skim milk

½ tsp garlic powder

½ tsp onion powder

½ tsp dried oregano

½ tsp salt

¼ tsp black pepper

½ cup (56 g) plus 2 tbsp (14 g) shredded part-skim mozzarella cheese, divided

6 tbsp (54 g) coarsely chopped turkey pepperoni, divided

Preheat the oven to 350°F (177°C). Spray a muffin tin with cooking spray.

Heat the oil in a medium skillet over medium-high heat. Add the spinach and cook it for 2 to 3 minutes, until it is bright green and soft.

In a medium bowl, whisk together the eggs, spaghetti sauce, milk, garlic powder, onion powder, oregano, salt, and black pepper.

Divide the cooked spinach, ½ cup (56 g) of the mozzarella cheese, and 4 tablespoons (36 g) of the pepperoni among the 12 muffin wells. Pour the egg mixture into the muffin wells. Sprinkle the eggs with the remaining 2 tablespoons (14 g) of mozzarella cheese and 2 tablespoons (18 g) of pepperoni.

Bake the mini frittatas for 18 to 22 minutes, until they are puffed up and cooked through.

Recipe Blueprint: *Using a base of 9 eggs and ¼ cup (60 ml) of milk, you can make any kind of mini frittatas you like. Make sure to cook your veggies first for the best results and don't be afraid to try all kinds of flavor combos.*

Pumpkin–Chocolate Chip Muffins (B)

I will happily eat pumpkin all year long, especially since it is a great way to add sweetness and moisture to baked goods without needing lots of sugar or oil. This hybrid of a muffin and baked oatmeal is full of warm spices, good-for-you ingredients, and just enough chocolate to taste like a treat.

Serves: 6

Total Time: 30 minutes

2 eggs

½ cup (113 g) pumpkin puree

⅓ cup (80 ml) skim milk or almond milk

3 tbsp (45 ml) pure maple syrup

1 tsp baking powder

¾ tsp pumpkin pie spice

½ tsp pure vanilla extract

¼ tsp ground cinnamon

¼ tsp salt

1 cup (80 g) old-fashioned oats

1 carrot, finely shredded

⅓ cup (60 g) chocolate chips

Preheat the oven to 375°F (191°C). Spray 6 wells of a 12-well muffin tin with cooking spray.

In a large bowl, whisk together the eggs, pumpkin puree, milk, maple syrup, baking powder, pumpkin pie spice, vanilla, cinnamon, and salt.

Add the oats to the egg mixture and stir well. Fold in the carrot and chocolate chips.

Divide the muffin batter among the wells of the prepared muffin tin.

Bake the muffins for 18 to 22 minutes, until a toothpick inserted into the center of a muffin comes out clean.

Leftover Love: *These muffins freeze well, so consider making a double or triple batch to have extra on hand. They make a great addition to lunches. Add them frozen in the morning and they are perfectly defrosted by lunchtime.*

Ultimate Breakfast Scramble (C)

This is a quick and easy breakfast scramble packed with crispy potatoes, tender spinach, and tasty chicken sausage. By using chicken sausage as the base, you can add flavor to the whole dish without needing lots of extra ingredients. And a little cheese makes everything better.

Serves: 2

Total Time: 15 minutes

4 eggs

2 tbsp (30 ml) skim milk

Salt, as needed

Black pepper, as needed

2 chicken sausages, coarsely chopped

1 cup (130 g) shredded hash brown potatoes

1 cup (30 g) baby spinach

¼ cup (28 g) shredded part-skim mozzarella cheese

In a medium bowl, whisk together the eggs, milk, salt, and black pepper. Set the egg mixture aside.

Heat a medium nonstick skillet over medium-high heat. Add the sausage in a single layer and cook it for 4 to 5 minutes, until it is browned. Push the sausage to one side of the skillet and add the potatoes. Press the potatoes down into the skillet and cook them for 3 to 4 minutes, until they are brown and crispy. Add the spinach, stirring the mixture to combine, and cook the mixture for 1 to 2 minutes, until the spinach is wilted. Remove the sausage, potatoes, and spinach from the skillet and set them aside.

Wipe the skillet clean and let it cool slightly. Spray it with cooking spray and place it over medium-high heat. Add the eggs and gently scramble them, being careful not to over-stir. Cook the eggs 2 to 3 minutes, until they are almost fully cooked, then add the sausage, potatoes, and spinach and fold them into the eggs.

Top the scramble with the mozzarella cheese and cover the skillet. Cook the scramble for 2 to 3 minutes, until the cheese melts and the eggs are cooked to your liking.

Recipe Blueprint: *By the time the weekend hits, I often make a hearty breakfast scramble to use up any remaining veggies and protein in the fridge. It's a great way to minimize food waste and can be made with any combination of veggies, protein, and cheese.*

Mason Jar Instant Lasagna Soup (D)

Most store-bought instant noodle soups are not at all healthy. Instead, make your own instant soup at home and fill it up with good-for-you ingredients. This lasagna-inspired version of instant soup is easy to make, packed with veggies and lean protein, and has all the flavors of a classic lasagna.

Serves: 4

Total Time: 20 minutes

2 cups (280 g) white or whole-wheat pasta

1⅓ cups (320 ml) spaghetti sauce

6 tsp (18 g) chicken bouillon

4 tsp (20 g) tomato paste

2 tsp (4 g) garlic powder

2 tsp (2 g) Italian seasoning

1 tsp black pepper

1 tsp red pepper flakes (optional)

2 cooked chicken sausages, finely chopped

1⅓ cups (200 g) shredded zucchini (about 1 zucchini)

4 tbsp (32 g) part-skim ricotta cheese

4 tbsp (28 g) shredded part-skim mozzarella cheese

Cook the pasta in boiling water until it is al dente. Immediately drain and rinse the pasta under cold water to stop the cooking process.

Set out 4 pint (473-ml) Mason jars. To each jar, add ⅓ cup (80 ml) of spaghetti sauce, 1½ teaspoons (5 g) of bouillon, 1 teaspoon of tomato paste, ½ teaspoon of garlic powder, ½ teaspoon of Italian seasoning, ¼ teaspoon of black pepper, and ¼ teaspoon of red pepper flakes (if using). Stir the ingredients together.

In layers, add the sausage, pasta, zucchini, ricotta cheese, and mozzarella cheese.

When ready to serve, fill each Mason jar with water and microwave the soup for 3 to 4 minutes, until it is hot.

Recipe Ideas: *Get creative and build all kinds of delicious DIY instant noodle soups. Start with a flavor base using bouillon (I prefer the paste) and spices. Then add par-cooked noodles. Finish with cooked protein and veggies. Then simply add water when you are ready to eat.*

Slow Cooker Honey-Soy Chicken (E)

This addictive Asian chicken dish with a sticky honey-soy sauce tastes just as good as takeout, but it is better for your wallet and waistline. Make sure to take the time to thicken the sauce so that it coats every bite of chicken.

Serves: 6

Total Time: 4 hours, 35 minutes

2 lb (900 g) boneless, skinless chicken thighs, trimmed

½ cup (120 ml) low-sodium soy sauce

¼ cup (60 ml) honey

2 tbsp (30 ml) rice vinegar

½ red onion, diced

4 cloves garlic, minced

1 tbsp (3 g) minced fresh ginger

1 tbsp (15 ml) Asian garlic chili paste (optional)

2 tbsp (18 g) cornstarch

¼ cup (13 g) sliced green onions

Add the chicken thighs to the slow cooker.

In a medium bowl, mix together the soy sauce, honey, vinegar, red onion, garlic, ginger, and Asian garlic chili paste (if using). Pour the sauce over the chicken. Cook the chicken on low for 4 hours.

Remove the chicken and set it aside. Whisk the cornstarch into the liquid in the slow cooker. Cover the slow cooker with its lid and increase the heat to high. Cook the sauce for 15 to 30 minutes, until it thickens to your liking.

Meanwhile, slice or shred the chicken. Transfer it back to the sauce. Top the chicken with the green onions.

Kitchen Hack: *If you forget to throw this in your slow cooker, you can always speed things up with a rotisserie chicken. Simply add the ingredients for the sauce to a small pot over medium heat and simmer it until it thickens. Then toss the sauce with the sliced rotisserie chicken and serve.*

Coconut Quinoa (F)

Sometimes just a few simple ingredients can completely transform a recipe. Take this dish: Quinoa is transformed with the addition of coconut. The quinoa comes out sweet, nutty, and anything but plain. It's the perfect side for Asian-inspired dishes.

Serves: 4

Total Time: 27 minutes

1½ tsp (8 g) coconut oil

⅔ cup (113 g) quinoa

2½ tbsp (13 g) unsweetened shredded coconut

1 cup (240 ml) canned coconut milk

⅓ cup (80 ml) water

1 tsp brown sugar or honey

¼ tsp kosher salt

Heat the coconut oil in a medium pot over medium-high heat. Add the quinoa and coconut. Toast them for 4 to 5 minutes, stirring often, until they are light brown. Add the coconut milk, water, brown sugar, and salt.

Bring the quinoa to a boil and stir. Reduce the heat to low. Cover the quinoa and cook it for 15 minutes.

Without uncovering the pot, turn off the heat and let the quinoa sit for 5 minutes, or until it is fluffy and the liquid is absorbed. Fluff the quinoa with a fork.

Make It Your Own: *We love adding some fresh lime juice to this dish, along with either chopped fresh cilantro or green onions. If you prefer something sweeter, use sweetened shredded coconut in place of the unsweetened. Trying to sneak in veggies? Throw in some cauliflower rice. It blends right in with the quinoa.*

Spicy Asian Brussels Sprouts (G)

The first time I made these Brussels sprouts, my husband and I literally ate the entire tray before it ever made it to the table, fighting over the crispy, almost-burnt bits. Don't be afraid to let these truly crisp up and caramelize—that's what makes them addictively delicious.

Serves: 2

Total Time: 27 minutes

8 oz (224 g) fresh Brussels sprouts, halved

½ tbsp (8 ml) sesame oil

Salt, as needed

Black pepper, as needed

1½ tbsp (23 ml) low-sodium soy sauce

1 tbsp (15 ml) honey

1 tsp rice vinegar

½ tsp Asian garlic chili paste, or as needed

¼ tsp garlic powder

Preheat the oven to 450°F (232°C). Spray a large baking sheet with cooking spray.

In a large bowl, toss the Brussels sprouts with the oil. Lightly season them with the salt and black pepper. Place the Brussels sprouts in a single layer on the baking sheet, leaving some space between the Brussels sprouts. They shouldn't overlap. Roast the Brussels sprouts for 20 to 25 minutes, or until they are brown and crispy.

Meanwhile, in a small saucepan over medium heat, combine the soy sauce, honey, rice vinegar, Asian garlic chili paste, and garlic powder. Bring the mixture to a simmer and cook it for 3 to 4 minutes, until it thickens and coats the back of a spoon. Remove the sauce from the heat.

Toss the hot Brussels sprouts with the sauce and serve.

Picky Eaters: *Brussels sprouts have a bad reputation as being something kids automatically hate, but my kids devour them when they are crispy, like they are in this recipe. If your kids don't like spice, leave some sprouts on the side without the sauce and serve some teriyaki sauce for dipping. This recipe will also work with carrots, cauliflower, or green beans if Brussels sprouts won't fly.*

Creamy Spinach and Artichoke Pasta (H)

Here is everything you love about spinach and artichoke dip rolled into an easy, lightened-up pasta dish. The trick is cooking the pasta in the sauce, so that the starch from the pasta can create a thick, rich sauce without the need for lots of cream.

Serves: 2

Total Time: 30 minutes

½ tbsp (8 ml) olive oil

8 oz (224 g) boneless, skinless chicken breast, thinly sliced

1 tsp grill seasoning

½ shallot, diced

2 cloves garlic, minced

1 cup (168 g) canned or jarred artichoke hearts, drained and coarsely chopped

2 cups (480 ml) low-sodium chicken broth

2 cups (280 g) pasta

2 cups (60 g) baby spinach

2 tbsp (10 g) shredded Parmesan cheese

2 tbsp (30 g) reduced-fat cream cheese

Salt, as needed

Black pepper, as needed

Heat the oil in a large pot over medium-high heat. Season the chicken with grill seasoning and add the chicken to the pot. Cook the chicken for 5 to 7 minutes, until it is brown and just cooked through. Remove the chicken and set it aside.

Add the shallot, garlic, and artichoke hearts to the pot. Cook for 3 to 4 minutes, stirring often.

Add the broth and bring the mixture to a boil. Add the pasta. Bring the mixture back to a boil, and then reduce the heat to medium-low. Cover the pot and cook the pasta for 12 to 15 minutes, stirring halfway through the cooking time, until the pasta is al dente and has absorbed most of the liquid.

Stir in the spinach and cook until it wilts. Stir in the Parmesan cheese, cream cheese, and cooked chicken. Remove the pot from the heat and let the mixture rest for 5 minutes to allow the sauce to thicken. Season the pasta with the salt and black pepper.

Picky Eaters: *Artichoke and spinach can be tricky ingredients for some kids. Mine are obsessed with the dip, so as long as I sell it that way, they will gobble it down. If your kids are pickier, simply substitute a vegetable they enjoy—peas, broccoli, cauliflower, or asparagus would all work.*

Broiled Barbecue Flank Steak with Mango Salsa (I)

Anytime we end up with last-minute dinner guests, you can almost guarantee I am making this meal. The presentation is beautiful, the flavors are complex, and the dish feels like it's something special. Little do our guests know that it actually couldn't be easier to make.

Serves: 4

Total Time: 25 minutes

Steak

1⅓ lb (600 g) lean flank steak

1 tbsp (15 ml) olive oil

1 tbsp (9 g) brown sugar

1½ tsp (3 g) paprika

1½ tsp (3 g) garlic powder

1 tsp onion powder

¾ tsp kosher salt

½ tsp chili powder

¼ tsp black pepper

Mango Salsa

1 mango, diced

1 jalapeño, diced (optional)

2 tbsp (18 g) diced red onion

2 tbsp (6 g) coarsely chopped fresh cilantro

Juice of 1 lime

Salt, as needed

Black pepper, as needed

To make the steak, preheat the oven to broil. Line a large baking sheet with foil.

Brush both sides of the steak with the oil.

In a small bowl, mix together the brown sugar, paprika, garlic powder, onion powder, salt, chili powder, and black pepper. Set the spice rub aside.

Place the steak on the foil-lined baking sheet. Broil the steak for 4 to 5 minutes. Carefully flip the steak over and cover the top with the spice rub. Broil the steak for 4 to 5 minutes, until it is brown and its internal temperature reaches 140°F (60°C) for medium doneness. Adjust the cooking time depending on your desired level of doneness. Remove the steak from the oven and tent it with foil. Let the steak rest for 10 minutes.

Meanwhile, make the mango salsa. In a medium bowl, mix together the mango, jalapeño (if using), onion, cilantro, lime juice, salt, and black pepper.

Slice the steak very thinly against the grain and serve it with the mango salsa.

Kitchen Tip: *During spring and summer, we make this dish on the grill. It will take the same amount of time on a medium-hot grill. For something extra special, toss your mango on the grill for a couple of minutes to add some smoky flavors.*

Steak Cooking Times

Rare— 4–6 minutes total

Medium Rare— 6–8 minutes total

Medium— 8–11 minutes total

Medium Well— 10–12 minutes total

Well— 12–15 minutes total

Cilantro-Lime Cauliflower Rice and Beans (J)

While my family may complain about plain cauliflower rice as a side dish, they devour this Cuban-inspired version. Pairing the cauliflower rice with hearty black beans, zesty cilantro, and bright lime juice transforms the cauliflower rice into a dish everyone loves.

Serves: 4

Total Time: 20 minutes

1 tsp olive oil

2 cups (650 g) fresh or frozen cauliflower rice

2 cloves garlic, minced

14 oz (392 g) canned black beans, drained and rinsed

¼ tsp ground cumin

¼ tsp dried oregano

2 to 4 tbsp (6 to 12 g) finely chopped fresh cilantro

Juice of 1 lime

Salt, as needed

Black pepper, as needed

Heat the oil in a large skillet over medium-high heat. Add the cauliflower rice and cook it for 4 to 5 minutes, until it is tender. Add the garlic and cook it for 30 seconds, until it is fragrant.

Stir in the black beans, cumin, and oregano. Cook the beans for 2 to 3 minutes, until they are heated through.

Turn off the heat and add the cilantro and lime juice. Season the beans with the salt and black pepper to taste.

Kitchen Hack: *On a busy weeknight, making homemade cauliflower rice can feel like too much. Instead, grab a bag of frozen, fresh, or shelf-stable cauliflower rice to speed things up.*

Skillet Pork Tenderloin with Apples and Snap Peas (K)

When I was growing up, my family never ate pork without apples. In fact, we begged for the cinnamon applesauce my mom always served with her grilled pork chops. This recipe is inspired by those meals but updated with delicious cooked apples and crispy snap peas.

Serves: 4

Total Time: 35 minutes

1⅓ lb (600 g) lean pork tenderloin, trimmed

1½ tbsp (9 g) grill seasoning

2 apples, peeled and diced

2 tsp (10 ml) honey

½ tsp ground cinnamon

Salt, as needed

2 cups (300 g) snap peas, trimmed

4 tsp (20 ml) olive oil, divided

Black pepper, as needed

Preheat the oven to 400°F (204°C).

Coat all sides of the pork with the grill seasoning. In a medium bowl, toss the apples with the honey, cinnamon, and a pinch of salt. In another medium bowl, toss the snap peas with 2 teaspoons (10 ml) of the oil, salt, and black pepper.

In a large, heavy, oven-safe skillet, heat the remaining 2 teaspoons (10 ml) of oil over medium-high heat. Add the pork tenderloin and sear the pork for 3 to 4 minutes on each side, turning the pork once it is brown. Push the pork to the center of the skillet. Add the snap peas on one side and the apples on the other side.

Place the skillet in the oven and roast the pork, apples, and snap peas for 13 to 17 minutes, or until the pork's internal temperature reaches 145°F (63°C). Stir the apples and snap peas halfway through the cooking time.

Tent the entire skillet with foil and let the pork rest for 10 minutes before serving.

Make It Yours: *This is one of those recipes that allows you to play with flavors. Use peaches, plums, or pears instead of apples. Swap out the spice blend for herbs like rosemary or thyme. Try different veggies like asparagus or green beans.*

Sheet-Pan Pesto Meatballs, Roasted Tomatoes, and Gnocchi (L)

These Italian-inspired gnocchi and meatballs are everything I want in a weeknight meal. This dish is easy to make (especially if you prep the meatballs in advance), packed with veggies, and is healthy comfort food at its best—warm, inviting, and delicious.

Serves: 4

Total Time: 35 minutes

1 lb (450 g) lean ground chicken

1 cup (150 g) grated zucchini (about 1 zucchini), squeezed of all moisture

¼ cup (14 g) whole-wheat panko breadcrumbs

3 tbsp (48 g) store-bought pesto, divided

1 tbsp (14 g) tomato paste

1 egg

1½ tsp (8 g) salt, divided

1 tsp black pepper, divided

1 lb (450 g) Campari or Roma tomatoes, quartered

10 oz (280 g) potato gnocchi

1 tbsp (15 ml) olive oil

¼ cup (20 g) shredded Parmesan cheese

2 tbsp (6 g) finely chopped fresh basil

Preheat the oven to 400°F (204°C). Line two large baking sheets with foil and spray the foil with cooking spray.

In a large bowl, combine the chicken, zucchini, breadcrumbs, 2 tablespoons (32 g) of the pesto, tomato paste, egg, 1 teaspoon of the salt, and ½ teaspoon of the black pepper. Use your hands to combine the ingredients, mixing gently so as not to compress the meat. Measure out 1 heaping tablespoon (15 g) of the meat mixture and form it into a meatball. Place the meatballs on one of the prepared baking sheets.

In another large bowl, toss together the tomatoes and gnocchi with the remaining 1 tablespoon (16 g) of pesto, oil, remaining ½ teaspoon of salt, and remaining ½ teaspoon of black pepper. Spread out the tomatoes and gnocchi on the second prepared baking sheet.

Place both baking sheets in the oven and cook for 18 to 20 minutes, until the meatballs are cooked through. Remove the gnocchi and tomatoes from the oven. Increase the oven's temperature to broil and broil the meatballs for 2 minutes, until they are crispy on the outside.

Add the gnocchi, tomatoes, and all the juice from their baking sheet to a large bowl. Add the meatballs. Top everything with the Parmesan cheese and basil.

Picky Eaters: *If roasted tomatoes aren't going to fly in your home, simply serve this dish with your favorite jarred pasta sauce or some extra pesto.*

Tomato-Basil Fish (M)

For years, this was my go-to order at a local Italian restaurant, and I always assumed it was hard to make. One day, I finally convinced the chef to share the recipe—I couldn't believe how easy it was. This dish calls for simple ingredients that result in the most delicious flavors.

Serves: 2

Total Time: 20 minutes

½ tbsp (8 ml) olive oil

2 cloves garlic, minced

10 oz (280 g) canned San Marzano tomatoes

1 tbsp (15 g) butter

¼ cup (13 g) coarsely chopped fresh basil

10 oz (280 g) white fish (like cod)

½ tsp dried oregano

Salt, as needed

Black pepper, as needed

Heat the oil in a medium skillet over medium heat. Add the garlic and cook it for 30 seconds, until it is fragrant. Add the tomatoes, breaking them up with a wooden spoon. Add the butter and basil. Cook the mixture for 5 minutes, until the tomatoes begin to break down.

Meanwhile, season the fish with the oregano, salt, and black pepper.

Add the fish to the pan and cover it with the tomato sauce. Cover the pan and cook the fish for 10 to 12 minutes, until the fish is cooked through and flakes easily with a fork.

Know Your Ingredients: *San Marzano tomatoes are a type of tomato from Italy that tend to be sweeter and less acidic than standard tomatoes. They can make a big difference in the flavor of tomato sauces and in my opinion are worth the extra money. With that said, regular canned tomatoes will also work just fine in this dish.*

Lemon-Garlic Roasted Broccoli and Polenta (N)

It's hard to beat roasted, nutty broccoli paired with sweet corn polenta all topped with lemon juice and Parmesan cheese. Plus, you get an all-in-one side dish without the need for multiple pots and pans.

Serves: 2

Total Time: 30 minutes

2 cups (350 g) broccoli florets

1 (6-oz [168-g]) tube polenta, cut into ½-inch (1-cm)-thick slices

1 tbsp (15 ml) olive oil

1 tsp garlic powder

½ tsp onion powder

Salt, as needed

Black pepper, as needed

Juice of ½ lemon

1 tbsp (5 g) shredded Parmesan cheese

Preheat the oven to 425°F (218°C). Spray a large baking sheet with cooking spray.

In a large bowl, toss the broccoli and polenta rounds with the oil, garlic powder, onion powder, salt, and black pepper.

Place the broccoli and polenta on the prepared baking sheet, spreading everything out in a single layer. Bake the broccoli and polenta for 18 to 22 minutes, flipping them halfway through the cooking time, until the broccoli is crisp-tender and the polenta is crispy and golden brown.

Season the broccoli and polenta with the lemon juice and Parmesan cheese.

Kitchen Tip: *Many people miss out on the true deliciousness of roasted veggies by taking them out too early. Make sure to let your veggies get caramelized and browned to bring out their full flavor.*

Crispy Baked Sweet Potato Taquitos (O)

When it comes to vegetarian dishes, I love making Mexican-inspired meals. There is something about a taco, or a crispy taquito in this case, that makes everyone forget there isn't meat in the dish. The chorizo-inspired spices also add tons of flavor to the sweet potato and black bean filling of these crispy taquitos.

Serves: 2

Total Time: 30 minutes

Taquitos

1 tsp olive oil

¼ red onion, diced

1 clove garlic, minced

1 cup (150 g) diced sweet potatoes

¾ cup (45 g) canned black beans, drained and rinsed

⅔ cup (150 g) canned diced tomatoes with green chiles, undrained

¼ to ½ tsp chili powder

¼ tsp ground cumin

¼ tsp paprika

⅛ cup (30 ml) water

Juice of ½ lime

1 to 2 tbsp (3 to 6 g) finely chopped fresh cilantro

Salt, as needed

Black pepper, as needed

6 corn tortillas

Creamy Salsa Verde

½ cup (120 ml) salsa verde

½ avocado

2 tbsp (6 g) finely chopped fresh cilantro

Salt, as needed

Preheat the oven to 425°F (218°C). Spray a large baking sheet with cooking spray.

To make the taquitos, heat the oil in a large skillet over medium-high heat. Add the onion and cook it for 4 to 5 minutes, until it is soft. Add the garlic and cook the mixture for 30 seconds, until the garlic is fragrant. Add the sweet potatoes, black beans, tomatoes with green chiles, chili powder, cumin, and paprika. Stir the mixture and add the water. Reduce the heat to medium-low and cover the skillet. Cook the filling for 10 minutes. Uncover the skillet and stir the mixture. Cook the filling for 2 to 3 minutes, if needed, until the sweet potatoes are tender and beginning to break down. Add the lime juice and cilantro. Season the filling with salt and black pepper.

To assemble the taquitos, wrap 3 tortillas in a moist paper towel. Microwave them for 30 to 45 seconds to soften the tortillas. Add 1 rounded tablespoon (15 g) of the filling to each of the tortillas. Roll the tortillas and place them on the prepared baking sheet, seam side down. Repeat this process with the remaining tortillas. Spray the taquitos with cooking spray.

Bake the taquitos for 22 to 25 minutes, until their tops are crispy. If needed, increase the oven's temperature to broil and broil the taquitos for 1 to 2 minutes to brown the edges.

While the taquitos are baking, make the creamy salsa verde. In a blender, combine the salsa verde, avocado, and cilantro. Blend until the ingredients are smooth. Season the creamy salsa verde with salt. Serve it with the taquitos.

Kitchen Hack: *The most time-consuming part of this recipe is making the taquitos. For a quicker option, simply bake your own crispy taco shells in an oven preheated to 400°F (204°C) for 8 to 10 minutes while you make the filling.*

Mexican Fruit Salad (P)

In our house, we make two versions of this salad—one for kids and one for adults. The kids love the honey-lime dressing and are excited to try the jicama. The adults love the unexpected twist of cheese and chili powder on a fruit salad. It's so well loved that we have to bring it everywhere we go in the summer.

Serves: 2

Total Time: 10 minutes

1 Persian cucumber, finely chopped

1 cup (154 g) coarsely chopped watermelon

½ cup (130 g) finely chopped jicama

Juice of ½ lime

½ tbsp (8 ml) honey

Pinch of salt

2 tbsp (6 g) finely chopped fresh cilantro (optional)

2 tbsp (16 g) crumbled queso fresco cheese (optional)

2 tbsp (12 g) chili powder (optional)

In a large bowl, toss the cucumber, watermelon, and jicama with the lime juice, honey, and salt. Add the cilantro (if using), queso fresco cheese (if using), and chili powder (if using). Alternatively, serve the cilantro, queso fresco cheese, and chili powder on the side.

Know Your Ingredients: *Jicama is a crisp, slightly sweet root vegetable that is popular in Mexico and often thought of as a fruit. Kids love it for its sweet flavor and parents love it since it is packed with nutrients. Simply remove the peel with a vegetable peeler before serving.*

Week 3

You're on a roll! This week is all about fun family favorites made healthier. We've got Slow Cooker Four-Veggie Lasagna (page 114), Ham, Cheese, and Zucchini Breakfast Quesadillas (page 107), Sesame-Orange Chicken and Broccoli (page 129), Sheet-Pan Sausage, Potatoes, Peppers, and Onions (page 122), Blackened Fish Tacos with Mexican Corn Slaw (page 130), and even Chickpea Pizza (page 134). As you head into this week, think of one thing you can do to make cooking even easier this week. Maybe it's spending more time on meal prep, relying on a kitchen hack, or passing the cooking responsibilities to someone else for one night.

Weekly Calendar

	Breakfast	Lunch	Dinner
Sunday	Ham, Cheese, and Zucchini Breakfast Quesadillas (A, page 107) *with fresh fruit*	Crunchy Thai Peanut and Mango Salad (D, page 113)	Slow Cooker Four-Veggie Lasagna (E, page 114) *with Italian Chopped Salad (F, page 117)*
Monday	Cinnamon Apple and Pear Oatmeal (B, page 109)	Slow Cooker Four-Veggie Lasagna* (E, page 114) *with 1 cup (30 g) greens*	Creamy Ranch Chicken Bites (G, page 118) *with Roasted Ranch Butternut Squash and Asparagus (H, page 121)*
Tuesday	Ham, Cheese, and Zucchini Breakfast Quesadillas* (A, page 107) *with fresh fruit*	Crunchy Thai Peanut and Mango Salad* (D, page 113)	Sheet-Pan Sausage, Potatoes, Peppers, and Onions (I, page 122)
Wednesday	Cinnamon Apple and Pear Oatmeal* (B, page 109)	Slow Cooker Four-Veggie Lasagna* (E, page 114) *with 1 cup (30 g) greens*	Mini Meatloaves and Green Beans (J, page 125) *with Garlic Sweet Potato Wedges (K, page 126)*
Thursday	Ham, Cheese, and Zucchini Breakfast Quesadillas* (A, page 107) *with fresh fruit*	Mini Meatloaves and Green Beans* (J, page 125) *with Garlic Sweet Potato Wedges* (K, page 126)*	Sesame-Orange Chicken and Broccoli (L, page 129) *with ½ cup (80 g) cooked brown rice*
Friday	Cinnamon Apple and Pear Oatmeal* (B, page 109)	Sesame-Orange Chicken and Broccoli* (L, page 129) *with ½ cup (59 g) shelled edamame*	Blackened Fish Tacos with Mexican Corn Slaw (M, page 130) *with Shortcut Refried Beans (N, page 133)*
Saturday	Sheet-Pan Sweet Potato and Veggie Breakfast Hash (C, page 110) *with fresh fruit*	Blackened Fish Tacos with Mexican Corn Slaw* (M, page 130) *with ½ cup (80 g) cooked brown rice and ¼ avocado*	Chickpea Pizza (O, page 134) *with Simple Yogurt Caesar Salad (P, page 137)*

* Indicates leftovers

Shopping List

Dairy and Refrigerated Items

- 13 eggs (A, C, E, J)
- 1½ cups (180 g) shredded Cheddar cheese (A, N)
- 3 cups (720 ml) unsweetened almond milk (B)
- 15 oz (420 g) part-skim ricotta cheese (E)
- 2⅓ cups (260 g) shredded part-skim mozzarella cheese (E, F, O)
- ⅔ cup (53 g) shredded Parmesan cheese (E, G, P)
- 1 cup (250 g) plus 1 tbsp (16 g) Greek yogurt (G, M, P)
- ⅔ cup (160 ml) orange juice (L)
- ¼ cup (32 g) queso fresco cheese (M)
- ¼ cup (62 g) pico de gallo (N)

Produce

- Fresh fruit for breakfast (A, C)
- 2 zucchini (A, E)
- 3 pears (B)
- 3 apples (B)
- 1½ cups (150 g) Brussels sprouts (C)
- ¾ sweet onion (C, I)
- 3 sweet potatoes (C, K)
- 1 mango (D)
- 2 cups (134 g) Lacinato kale (D)
- 10 cloves garlic (D, E, I, J, L, N, P)
- 1½ red bell peppers (D, I)
- 1½ cups (75 g) carrots (D, J)
- ½ cup (25 g) cilantro (D, M)
- 2½ cups (850 g) coleslaw mix (D, M)
- 4 green onions (D, M)
- 1 cup (75 g) mushrooms (E)
- 4 cups (120 g) greens (E)
- 1 cup (30 g) baby spinach (E)
- 2½ cups (350 g) butternut squash (E, H)
- 1¼ onions (E, J, N)
- ½ cup (75 g) cherry tomatoes (F)
- 1 tbsp (3 g) parsley (F)
- 3 lemons (F, G, P)
- 5 cups (375 g) romaine lettuce (F, P)
- 8 spears asparagus (H)
- 1 potato (I)
- ½ green bell pepper (I)
- 3 cups (450 g) green beans (J)
- 1 orange (L)
- 4 cups (700 g) broccoli florets (L)
- 3 cups (750 g) corn (M)
- 1 lime (M)
- 2 avocados (M)
- 1 jalapeño (M)

Meat, Poultry, and Fish

- 1 cup (150 g) lean ham (A)
- 2 slices turkey bacon (C)
- 2 lb (900 g) boneless, skinless chicken breast (G, L)
- 2 sweet or spicy Italian turkey sausages (I)
- 1 lb (450 g) 93% lean ground turkey (J)
- 1 lb (450 g) cod (M)

Grains, Pasta, Bulk

- 6 flour tortillas (A)
- 2 cups (160 g) old-fashioned oats (B)
- 2 tbsp (20 g) chia seeds (B)
- 2 tbsp (14 g) flaxseed meal (B)
- ½ cup (85 g) quinoa (D)
- 12 white or whole-wheat lasagna noodles (E)
- 5½ cups (1.3 L) spaghetti sauce (E, O)
- 2 cups (320 g) cooked brown rice (L, M)
- 8 corn tortillas (M)
- 1 small sourdough roll (P)

Packaged, Canned, and Jarred Items

- 2 tbsp (30 ml) salsa verde (A)
- 4 tbsp (64 g) almond butter (B)
- 2 tbsp (22 g) peanut butter (D)
- 2 cups (236 g) shelled edamame (D, M)
- ¼ cup (83 g) canned chickpeas (F)
- 2 tbsp (18 g) pepperoncini (F)
- 2 tbsp (22 g) black olives (F)
- 1 cup (169 g) canned pinto beans (N)
- ½ cup (120 ml) chicken broth (N)

(Continued)

Shopping List (Continued)

Pantry Spices

- Onion powder (A)
- Ground cinnamon (B)
- Ground ginger (B, L)
- Garlic powder (C, K, O)
- Italian seasoning (E, F, I, O)
- Grill seasoning (J)
- Dried basil (K)
- Blackening seasoning (M)
- Kosher salt

Refrigerated

- Low-sodium soy sauce (D, L)
- Ranch dressing (H)

- Dijon mustard (I)
- Ketchup (J)
- Yellow mustard (J)
- Worcestershire sauce (J, P)
- Light mayonnaise (M)

Other Items

- Olive oil (A, C, F, H, M, O, P)
- Pure vanilla extract (B)
- Pure maple syrup (B, D)
- Sesame oil (D, L)
- Rice vinegar (D, L)
- Red wine vinegar (F)
- 2 tbsp (12 g) ranch seasoning (G, H)

- ⅔ cup (66 g) whole-wheat seasoned breadcrumbs (J)
- Brown sugar (J)
- Cornstarch (L)
- Honey (L)
- Sesame seeds (L)
- 1 cup (130 g) chickpea flour (O)
- ½ to 1 cup (120 to 240 g) pizza toppings of choice (O)
- ¼ tsp anchovy paste (P)
- Cooking spray

Game Plan

This week, there are multiple opportunities to take shortcuts by using the kitchen hacks included in the following lists. If you have an especially busy week, don't shy away from taking the easy road.

Meal Prep

- Prepare the overnight-oats option of the Cinnamon Apple and Pear Oatmeal (B, page 109), if using.

- Make the quinoa and dressing for the Crunchy Thai Peanut and Mango Salad (D, page 113).

- Make the dressing for the Italian Chopped Salad (F, page 117).

- Make the Mini Meatloaves (J, page 125) and store them in the fridge or freezer.

- Make the sauce for the Sesame-Orange Chicken and Broccoli (L, page 129).

- Make the brown rice for the Sesame-Orange Chicken and Broccoli (L, page 129) and the leftover Blackened Fish Tacos with Mexican Corn Slaw (M, page 130).

- Make the dressing for the Simple Yogurt Caesar Salad (P, page 137).

- Prep the produce like so:

  - **Brussels sprouts:** 1½ cups (150 g), quartered (C, page 110)

  - **Sweet onion:** ¼ onion, diced (C, page 110); ½ onion, cut into ½-inch (13-mm)-thick slices (I, page 122)

  - **Lacinato kale:** 2 cups (134 g), coarsely chopped (D, page 113)

  - **Red bell pepper:** 1 pepper, coarsely chopped (D, page 113); ½ pepper, cut into ½-inch (1-cm)-thick slices (I, page 122)

  - **Butternut squash:** 1 cup (140 g), diced (E, page 114); 2 cups (280 g) coarsely chopped, cut into ½-inch (1-cm) cubes (H, page 121)

  - **Green bell pepper:** ½ pepper, cut into ½-inch (1-cm)-thick slices (I, page 122)

  - **Onion:** ½ cup (72 g), grated (J, page 125); ¼ cup (36 g), diced (N, page 133)

  - **Carrots:** ½ cup (25 g), finely shredded (J, page 125)

  - **Broccoli:** 4 cups (700 g) florets (L, page 129)

  - Prep fruit for breakfasts

  - Measure out greens and edamame for lunches

- Freeze the chicken breast and cod if needed.

Daily Tips

- **Sunday:** Start the Slow Cooker Four-Veggie Lasagna (E, page 114) at least 3 hours before dinner.

- **Monday:** Get the butternut squash in the oven, then marinate the chicken. Place the ranch chicken and asparagus in the oven at the same time.

- **Wednesday:** Start cooking the Mini Meatloaves (J, page 125) and Garlic Sweet Potato Wedges (K, page 126) at the same time. Place the chicken breast in the fridge to defrost, if needed.

- **Thursday:** If you are cooking brown rice from scratch, start it before the chicken since it normally takes longer. Place the fish in the fridge to defrost overnight.

- **Friday:** Make the Mexican Corn Slaw (M, page 130) first. Then prepare the Shortcut Refried Beans (N, page 133), since they will stay warm on the stove. Cook the fish last.

- **Saturday:** Make the dressing before starting the pizza, so that there is time for the flavors to blend before serving.

- **Sunday:** Buy a healthy premade Italian dressing instead of making your own, or buy a whole prepared salad.

- **Monday:** Buy the precut butternut squash in the produce section.

- **Wednesday:** Grab frozen baked sweet potato or veggie fries instead of making your own.

- **Thursday:** Make the orange sauce on the stove and toss it with rotisserie chicken and frozen broccoli. Grab frozen or precooked brown rice.

- **Friday:** Skip the homemade corn slaw and mix together store-bought pico de gallo, canned corn, and avocado for the salsa. Buy canned refried beans.

- **Saturday:** Pick up some fresh pizza dough or a premade crust for the pizza. Grab a bottle of yogurt-based Caesar dressing and a bag of baked croutons for the salad.

Ham, Cheese, and Zucchini Breakfast Quesadillas (A)

Portable breakfasts are an absolute necessity in our home since someone is always running out the door five minutes late. These hearty quesadillas can be kept in the freezer for a quick and healthy breakfast that can be eaten on the go.

Serves: 6

Total Time: 25 minutes

8 eggs

2 tbsp (30 ml) salsa verde (optional)

¾ tsp salt, or as needed

½ tsp black pepper

½ tsp onion powder

1 tsp olive oil

1 zucchini, grated

1 cup (150 g) diced lean ham

1 cup (120 g) plus 2 tbsp (16 g) shredded Cheddar cheese

6 flour tortillas

In a medium bowl, whisk together the eggs, salsa verde (if using), salt, black pepper, and onion powder.

Heat the oil in a large skillet over medium-high heat. Add the zucchini and cook it for 3 to 4 minutes, until it has softened. Add the ham and cook the mixture for 1 minute. Reduce the heat to medium. Slowly pour in the egg mixture. Slowly scramble the eggs as they firm up on the edges and bottom of the skillet. Cook the eggs, stirring gently, for 4 to 6 minutes, until they are just set. Be careful not to overcook them.

Assemble the quesadillas by placing 1½ tablespoons (28 g) of Cheddar cheese on half of a tortilla. Add some of the eggs and ham and another 1½ tablespoons (28 g) of Cheddar cheese. Fold the empty half of the tortilla on top of the filling. Repeat these steps with the remaining tortillas.

Spray a large nonstick skillet with cooking spray. Heat the skillet over medium-high heat. Add the quesadillas and cook them for 3 to 4 minutes per side, until they are brown and the cheese is melted.

*See photo on page 100.

Storage and Reheating: *If you are making the quesadillas ahead of time, let them cool completely. Wrap them in plastic wrap and store them in the fridge or freezer. To reheat a quesadilla from the fridge, microwave the quesadilla for 1 to 1½ minutes, until the quesadilla is heated through. For best results, reheat the quesadilla in a skillet or the toaster oven for a crispy outside. To reheat a quesadilla from the freezer, wrap the quesadilla in a moist paper towel and microwave it for 1½ to 2½ minutes. For best results, finish it by toasting it in a toaster oven or skillet.*

Recipe Blueprint: *Normally, when we make breakfast quesadillas, it's a family affair—I let everyone build their own so we have lots of variety in the freezer. Simply scramble a bunch of eggs, set out the toppings and cheese, and create an assembly line. Use a large griddle to speed up the cooking time.*

Cinnamon Apple and Pear Oatmeal (B)

Ditch the sugar-filled instant oatmeal packets and make your own in about the same amount of time. This recipe starts with fresh fruit for natural sweetness and reminds me of my deep love for fall desserts. The almond butter adds some protein for staying power.

Serves: 1 (see note)

Total Time: 8 minutes

½ pear, coarsely chopped

½ apple, coarsely chopped

2 tbsp (30 ml) water

¼ tsp ground cinnamon, or as needed

⅛ tsp ground ginger

⅓ cup (27 g) old-fashioned oats

1 tsp chia seeds

1 tsp flaxseed meal

½ cup (120 ml) unsweetened almond milk

1 tsp pure maple syrup, or as needed

¼ tsp pure vanilla extract

2 tsp (10 g) almond butter

In a medium microwave-safe bowl, combine the pear, apple, water, cinnamon, and ginger. Microwave the mixture for 1½ to 2 minutes, until the fruit is soft. Alternatively, combine the ingredients in a medium saucepan over medium heat and cook them for 5 to 7 minutes.

Stir in the oats, chia seeds, and flaxseed meal. Add the milk, maple syrup, and vanilla. Stir well.

Microwave the oatmeal for 1½ minutes. Stir the oatmeal and microwave it for an additional 1½ to 2 minutes, until it is cooked through. Top the oatmeal with the almond butter.

Number of Servings: *To make this recipe easier to prepare, the ingredients are listed for one serving, but you will likely be preparing more than one serving.*

Recipe Ideas: *If you prefer to make this recipe in advance, turn it into overnight oats. Cook the apple and pear, then layer everything into a Mason jar and refrigerate the oatmeal overnight. This oatmeal keeps in the fridge for up to 5 days and can be served hot or cold.*

Sheet-Pan Sweet Potato and Veggie Breakfast Hash (C)

Hash is one of those dishes I reserved for mornings out—until I learned just how easy it is to make on a sheet pan. My favorite hash always has an unexpected vegetable, like Brussels sprouts. For a little sweetness, sometimes we add dried cranberries on top before serving.

Serves: 2

Total Time: 45 minutes

1 sweet potato, cubed

1½ cups (150 g) quartered Brussels sprouts

¼ sweet onion, diced

2 tsp (10 ml) olive oil

½ tsp garlic powder

Salt, as needed

Black pepper, as needed

2 slices turkey bacon, coarsely chopped

2 eggs

Preheat the oven to 425°F (218°C). Spray a medium baking sheet with cooking spray.

In a medium bowl, toss the sweet potato, Brussels sprouts, and onion with the oil, garlic powder, salt, and black pepper. Spread the vegetables on the prepared baking sheet in a single layer. Sprinkle the bacon on top of the vegetables.

Roast the vegetables and bacon for 25 to 30 minutes, until the potatoes are tender. Carefully remove the baking sheet from the oven. Arrange the vegetables to make two empty areas big enough for the eggs. Spray these areas with extra cooking spray. Crack an egg into each empty area. Season the eggs with salt and black pepper.

Return the baking sheet to the oven and cook for 3 to 6 minutes, until the eggs reach your desired level of doneness.

Picky Eaters: *Rather than combining the sweet potato and Brussels sprouts, cook the sweet potato on one side of the baking sheet and the Brussels sprouts on the other. Let your kids choose what they want and serve the dish with fresh fruit if they forego the Brussels sprouts. This recipe also works great with scrambled eggs, cooked separately, if needed.*

Crunchy Thai Peanut and Mango Salad (D)

Many times, we think we need to reach for meat to get protein in our salads. This salad uses quinoa, edamame, and a peanut butter–based dressing to add lots of protein without meat. Inspired by our favorite farmers market Buddha bowl, this salad is hard to put down.

Serves: 4

Total Time: 40 minutes

Dressing

1 green onion

½ clove garlic

¼ cup (60 ml) low-sodium soy sauce

2 tbsp (22 g) peanut butter

2 tbsp (30 ml) hot water

1 tbsp (15 ml) sesame oil

1 tbsp (15 ml) pure maple syrup

1 tbsp (15 ml) rice vinegar

Salad

½ cup (85 g) quinoa

1 cup (240 ml) water

2 cups (680 g) coleslaw mix

2 cups (134 g) coarsely chopped Lacinato kale

1 red bell pepper, coarsely chopped

1 cup (118 g) edamame

1 cup (50 g) shredded carrots

1 mango, coarsely chopped

¼ cup (13 g) finely chopped fresh cilantro

2 green onions, finely chopped

To make the dressing, combine the green onion, garlic, soy sauce, peanut butter, water, oil, maple syrup, and vinegar in a blender. Blend until the dressing is smooth. If needed, thin out the dressing with extra water.

To make the salad, combine the quinoa and water in a small saucepan over medium-high heat. Bring the quinoa to a boil and stir it. Reduce the heat to low and cover the saucepan. Cook the quinoa for 15 minutes. Remove the saucepan from the heat without uncovering it. Let the quinoa rest for 5 minutes, until it is fluffy and tender. Fluff it with a fork, then let the quinoa cool completely. To hasten cooling, spread out the quinoa on a medium baking sheet.

In a large bowl, toss together the quinoa, coleslaw mix, kale, bell pepper, edamame, carrots, mango, cilantro, and green onions. Drizzle the dressing on top of the salad. Store any extra dressing in the fridge for up to 2 weeks.

Picky Eaters: *Salad can be tough for some children, so try serving these as build-your-own Asian tacos or lettuce wraps. Set the ingredients out and encourage everyone to try at least one new veggie.*

Slow Cooker Four-Veggie Lasagna (E)

Many people shy away from cooking lasagna in the slow cooker after experiencing soupy, watery lasagna one too many times. The key to making perfect slow cooker lasagna is to precook your veggies and—most important—to let the lasagna rest for at least 30 minutes before serving, which allows it to firm up.

Serves: 6

Total Time: 3 hours and 45 minutes

2 tsp (10 ml) olive oil

½ onion, diced

1 cup (75 g) diced mushrooms

1 cup (30 g) finely chopped baby spinach

1 cup (124 g) diced zucchini

1 cup (140 g) diced butternut squash

3 cloves garlic, minced

15 oz (420 g) part-skim ricotta cheese

1½ cups (168 g) shredded part-skim mozzarella cheese, divided

⅓ cup (27 g) shredded Parmesan cheese

1 tbsp (3 g) Italian seasoning

1 egg

Salt, as needed

Black pepper, as needed

5 cups (1.2 L) spaghetti sauce

12 white or whole-wheat lasagna noodles

Heat the oil in a large skillet over medium-high heat. Add the onion, mushrooms, spinach, zucchini, butternut squash, and garlic. Cook the vegetables for 6 to 8 minutes, until they are tender. Drain any excess moisture. Let the vegetables cool.

In a medium bowl, mix together the ricotta cheese, vegetables mixture, 1 cup (112 g) of the mozzarella cheese, Parmesan cheese, Italian seasoning, egg, salt, and black pepper.

Spray the insert of a slow cooker with cooking spray. Add 1½ cups (360 ml) of the spaghetti sauce to the bottom of the slow cooker. Then add a layer of 3 lasagna noodles, breaking them up as needed to fit. (It's okay if they overlap slightly.) Spoon one-third of the ricotta mixture on top of the noodles, spreading it out with a spoon. Add 1 cup (240 ml) of spaghetti sauce and spread it out with a spoon. Repeat with two more layers of noodles, ricotta cheese mixture, and sauce. Finish the lasagna with 3 more noodles. Pour ½ cup (120 ml) of spaghetti sauce on top.

Cook the lasagna on high for 3 hours or on low for 5 to 6 hours. Turn off the heat. Open the slow cooker and sprinkle the remaining ½ cup (56 g) of mozzarella cheese on top of the lasagna. Cover the slow cooker with its lid. Let the lasagna sit for at least 30 minutes (or preferably 60 minutes) before serving to allow the lasagna to firm up.

Recipe Ideas: *This lasagna can be made with any combination of cooked veggies you like. You can also add browned beef, turkey, or sausage. Mix it right into the spaghetti sauce.*

Italian Chopped Salad (F)

Inspired by my very favorite pizza place's salad, this classic salad is crunchy, tangy, and balanced. It's also the salad that started my oldest daughter on salads, although I will admit there was some pizza bribery involved. These days, she happily gobbles this up with any meal.

Serves: 2

Total Time: 10 minutes

Salad

2 cups (150 g) coarsely chopped romaine lettuce

½ cup (75 g) cherry tomatoes

¼ cup (41 g) canned chickpeas, drained and rinsed

2 tbsp (18 g) coarsely chopped pepperoncini

2 tbsp (22 g) coarsely chopped black olives

2 tbsp (14 g) shredded part-skim mozzarella cheese

1 tbsp (3 g) finely chopped fresh parsley

Kosher salt, as needed

Black pepper, as needed

Dressing

1½ tbsp (23 ml) olive oil

½ tbsp (8 ml) pepperoncini brine

½ tbsp (8 ml) fresh lemon juice

½ tbsp (8 ml) red wine vinegar

½ tsp Italian seasoning

To make the salad, toss together the lettuce, tomatoes, chickpeas, pepperoncini, olives, mozzarella cheese, and parsley in a large bowl.

To make the dressing, whisk together the oil, pepperoncini brine, lemon juice, vinegar, and Italian seasoning in a small bowl.

Add the dressing to the salad and toss to combine. Season the salad with the salt and black pepper.

Make It Your Own: *Everyone has their favorite version of this salad, so make it match yours. Add chopped salami, capers, or red onions, or swap in a creamy Italian dressing.*

Creamy Ranch Chicken Bites (G)

"Everything tastes better with ranch" is a philosophy I can fully get behind, and this family-favorite chicken is evidence of that. The Greek yogurt marinade ensures a tender and flavor-packed chicken. No one would blame you for drizzling some Buffalo sauce right on top.

Serves: 2

Total Time: 30 minutes

10 oz (280 g) boneless, skinless chicken breast, cut into bite-size pieces

¼ cup (63 g) Greek yogurt

2 tbsp (10 g) shredded Parmesan cheese

1 tbsp (6 g) homemade or store-bought ranch seasoning, divided (see note)

¼ tsp lemon zest

Salt, as needed

Black pepper, as needed

Preheat the oven to 400°F (204°C). Line a medium baking sheet with foil and spray the foil with cooking spray.

In a large bowl, stir together the chicken, yogurt, Parmesan cheese, ranch seasoning, and lemon zest. Marinate the chicken for at least 15 minutes (or up to 60 minutes) at room temperature.

Spread the chicken out in a single layer on the prepared baking sheet. Bake the chicken for 10 to 15 minutes, until the chicken's internal temperature reaches at least 165°F (74°C). Optionally, during the last 2 minutes of cooking time, increase the oven's temperature to broil to brown the top of the chicken.

Season the chicken with the salt and black pepper and serve.

Know Your Ingredients: *It's important to pay attention to the ingredients in store-bought ranch seasoning mixes, since some have lots of artificial and unnecessary ingredients. Look for a seasoning blend that contains dried buttermilk, dried herbs, and dried spices only. For the healthiest option, make your own by mixing the following: ¼ cup (60 g) dried buttermilk, 1½ tablespoons (9 g) onion powder, 1 tablespoon (6 g) garlic powder, ½ tablespoon (3 g) dried chives, ½ tablespoon (3 g) dried dill, ½ tablespoon (3 g) dried parsley, 2 teaspoons (5 g) kosher salt and ½ teaspoon black pepper.*

Roasted Ranch Butternut Squash and Asparagus (H)

One of the best strategies for introducing new foods is to pair it with something familiar, like the ranch seasoning in this recipe. The butternut squash gets caramelized and sweet, the asparagus gets nutty and delicious, and the herbal flavors in the ranch bring it all together.

Serves: 2

Total Time: 40 minutes

1½ cups (210 g) coarsely chopped butternut squash, cut into ½-inch (1-cm) cubes

1 tbsp (15 ml) olive oil, divided

1 tbsp (6 g) homemade or store-bought ranch seasoning, divided

8 spears asparagus

Salt, as needed

Black pepper, as needed

Ranch dressing (optional)

Preheat the oven to 400°F (204°C). Spray a large baking sheet with cooking spray.

In a medium bowl, toss the butternut squash with ½ tablespoon (8 ml) of the oil and ½ tablespoon (3 g) of the ranch seasoning. Spread the butternut squash out on the prepared baking sheet in a single layer. Roast the butternut squash for 20 minutes, until it is almost tender and is beginning to brown.

Meanwhile, in a medium bowl, toss the asparagus with the remaining ½ tablespoon (7 ml) of oil and ½ tablespoon (3 g) of ranch seasoning.

Push the butternut squash to one side of the baking sheet. Add the asparagus. Roast the butternut squash and asparagus for 10 to 12 minutes, until the butternut squash is tender and caramelized on the edges and the asparagus is bright green and crisp-tender. Season them with the salt and black pepper.

Serve the ranch dressing (if using) on the side for dipping or drizzling on top.

Kitchen Tip: *Struggling to peel the butternut squash? Start by piercing it all over with a fork, then cut off the ends. Microwave it for 3½ minutes. Once it is cool enough to handle, use a vegetable peeler to easily remove the skin.*

Sheet-Pan Sausage, Potatoes, Peppers, and Onions (I)

Sausage and pepper sandwiches are one of my favorite guilty pleasures, but with more than 850 calories, they are definitely an indulgence I save for the ballpark. At home, when that craving strikes, I love making this simple sheet-pan supper that my family devours. It has all the classic flavors but is lightened up with turkey sausages, roasted veggies, and a touch of mustard for that stadium flavor.

Serves: 2

Total Time: 45 minutes

1 potato, chopped into ½-inch (1-cm) pieces

½ green bell pepper, cut into ½-inch (1-cm)-thick slices

½ red bell pepper, cut into ½-inch (1-cm)-thick slices

½ sweet onion, cut into ½-inch (1-cm)-thick slices

2 cloves garlic, minced

1 tbsp (15 ml) olive oil

1 tbsp (16 g) Dijon mustard

1 tsp Italian seasoning

½ tsp salt

¼ tsp black pepper

2 sweet or spicy Italian turkey sausages (see note)

Preheat the oven to 400°F (204°C). Spray a large baking sheet with cooking spray.

In a large bowl, toss together the potato, green bell pepper, red bell pepper, onion, and garlic with the oil, mustard, Italian seasoning, salt, and black pepper. Stir until everything is combined and well coated.

Arrange the vegetables in a single layer on the prepared baking sheet. If needed, use two baking sheets to prevent the vegetables from overlapping. Roast the vegetables for 15 minutes.

Meanwhile, pierce the sausages with a fork. Carefully open the oven and arrange the sausages on top of the vegetables. Roast the vegetables and sausages for 17 to 22 minutes, until the sausages are light brown and their internal temperature reaches 165°F (74°C). Increase the oven's temperature to broil during the last 2 to 3 minutes of cooking time to brown the sausages, if desired.

Let the sausages rest for 2 minutes, then slice the sausages and serve.

Honey Mustard Drizzle: *For even more flavor, serve with some honey mustard to drizzle on top. Combine 2 tablespoons (32 g) of plain yogurt with 2 tablespoons (30 ml) of honey and 2 tablespoons (32 g) of Dijon mustard.*

Sausage Substitution: *If you prefer using precooked turkey sausage, slice it and add it during the last 10 minutes of cooking so it doesn't dry out.*

Kitchen Tip: *Do your roasted potatoes and vegetables come out without that wonderful, crispy brown exterior? You are probably overcrowding the pan. Give your veggies some room to breathe, even if that means using two baking sheets. The veggies will come out brown and delicious every time.*

Mini Meatloaves and Green Beans (J)

I'll be honest—I was never a meatloaf fan until I started making these flavor-packed mini meatloaves. It doesn't hurt that my kids are obsessed with them. They are everything meatloaf should be: moist, packed with flavor, and covered with a sticky, slightly sweet glaze. Plus, by making them individually sized, they cook in half the time.

Serves: 4

Total Time: 40 minutes

Mini Meatloaves and Green Beans

1 lb (450 g) 93% lean ground turkey

⅔ cup (66 g) seasoned whole-wheat breadcrumbs

½ cup (72 g) grated onion

½ cup (25 g) finely shredded carrots

2 cloves garlic, minced

2 tbsp (34 g) ketchup

2 tsp (4 g) grill seasoning, plus more if desired

1 egg

1 egg white

1 tsp Worcestershire sauce

Salt, as needed

Black pepper, as needed

3 cups (450 g) green beans

1 tbsp (15 ml) olive oil

Glaze

2 tbsp (34 g) ketchup

1 tsp brown sugar

1 tsp yellow mustard

Preheat the oven to 400°F (204°C). Line a large baking sheet with foil and spray the foil with cooking spray.

To make the meatloaves and green beans, combine the turkey, breadcrumbs, onion, carrots, garlic, ketchup, grill seasoning, egg, egg white, and Worcestershire sauce in a large bowl. Season the mixture with salt and black pepper as needed, depending on the grill seasoning used. Use your hands to gently combine the meatloaf mixture, being sure not to compress the meat. Divide the mixture into four portions. Use your hands to shape each portion into a mini meatloaf, not more than 1 inch (2.5 cm) thick. Place the meatloaves on the prepared baking sheet. Bake the meatloaves for 15 minutes.

Meanwhile, trim the green beans. Place them in another large bowl and toss them with the oil. Season them with salt, black pepper, and additional grill seasoning (if desired).

To make the glaze, mix together the ketchup, brown sugar, and mustard in a small bowl.

Remove the baking sheet from the oven. Brush the meatloaves with the glaze. Add the green beans to the baking sheet.

Return the baking sheet to the oven and cook the meatloaves and green beans for 10 to 12 minutes, until the meatloaves' internal temperature reaches 165°F (74°C) and the green beans are crisp-tender.

Recipe Blueprint: *Use this meatloaf recipe as a base and try out different flavor combinations. Add cheese and taco seasoning for a Mexican spin. Use Italian seasoning and spaghetti sauce for the glaze for an Italian option. Use different veggies to switch things up.*

Garlic Sweet Potato Wedges (K)

I am obsessed with these sweet potato wedges and may even like them more than sweet potato fries. The outside gets brown and crispy while the inside is tender and sweet. Usually, I eat my full serving before they even make it to the table.

Serves: 4

Total Time: 35 minutes

2 sweet potatoes, cut into thin wedges

1½ tbsp (23 ml) olive oil

¾ tsp garlic powder

½ tsp dried basil

½ tsp kosher salt, plus more as needed

Black pepper, as needed

Preheat the oven to 400°F (204°C). Spray a large baking sheet with cooking spray.

Toss the sweet potatoes with the oil, garlic powder, basil, salt, and black pepper on the prepared baking sheet. Spread the potatoes out in a single layer. Bake the wedges for 25 to 30 minutes, flipping them halfway through the cooking time, until the wedges are brown and crispy.

Know Your Ingredients: *There are more than sixteen varieties of sweet potatoes! Although any variety will work, I find the standard jewel sweet potato and extra sweet nugget sweet potato work best for roasting.*

Sesame-Orange Chicken and Broccoli (L)

This dish is a healthy mash-up of two take-out favorites—sesame chicken and orange chicken—but without all the deep-frying and sugar. This dish is easy to make and on constant rotation in our house.

Serves: 4

Total Time: 35 minutes

1⅓ lb (600 g) chicken, coarsely chopped

2 tbsp (18 g) cornstarch, divided

Salt, as needed

Black pepper, as needed

⅔ cup (160 ml) orange juice

3 tbsp (45 ml) low-sodium soy sauce

2 tbsp (30 ml) honey

1 tbsp (15 ml) rice vinegar

½ tsp ground ginger

2 cloves garlic, minced

Zest of 1 orange

1 tbsp (15 ml) sesame oil

4 cups (700 g) broccoli florets

1 tbsp (10 g) sesame seeds

Preheat the oven to 400°F (204°C).

In a large bowl, toss the chicken with 1 tablespoon (9 g) of the cornstarch, salt, and black pepper.

In a small bowl, whisk together the orange juice, soy sauce, honey, remaining 1 tablespoon (9 g) of cornstarch, vinegar, ginger, garlic, and orange zest. Set the mixture aside.

In a large oven-safe skillet, heat the oil over medium heat. Add the chicken in a single layer. Cook it for 2 to 3 minutes on one side, until it is brown. Flip the chicken and cook it for 2 to 3 minutes on the other side. Turn off the heat and pour the sauce mixture over the chicken, stirring to combine. Place the skillet in the oven and cook the chicken for 10 minutes.

Carefully remove the skillet and stir in the broccoli. Return the skillet to the oven and cook for 5 minutes. Sprinkle the chicken and broccoli with the sesame seeds and serve.

Kitchen Hack: *Miss the crunch? My friend makes this recipe for her kids all the time with store-bought baked chicken nuggets. She gets the nuggets and broccoli started on a baking sheet while she reduces the sauce on the stove until it's thick. Toss the sauce with the nuggets and broccoli for a healthier version that still has crispy chicken.*

Blackened Fish Tacos with Mexican Corn Slaw (M)

For years, every Friday afternoon after work I would treat myself to a fish taco and giant cob of Mexican street corn. Taking inspiration from that delicious meal, I love making these spicy tacos with creamy corn slaw to welcome the weekend. This dish is quick, easy, and so good.

Serves: 4

Total Time: 25 minutes

Mexican Corn Slaw

½ tbsp (8 ml) olive oil

3 cups (750 g) fresh, canned, or frozen corn

3 tbsp (42 g) light mayonnaise

2 tbsp (32 g) plain Greek yogurt

Juice and zest of 1 lime

Salt, as needed

Black pepper, as needed

1 avocado, coarsely chopped

½ cup (170 g) coleslaw mix

¼ cup (13 g) finely chopped fresh cilantro

1 jalapeño, minced (seeds removed for less spice)

1 green onion, minced

¼ cup (32 g) crumbled queso fresco cheese

Tacos

1 tbsp (6 g) blackening seasoning

1 lb (450 g) cod

1 tbsp (15 ml) olive oil

8 corn tortillas, warmed

To make the Mexican corn slaw, heat the oil in a medium heavy-bottomed skillet over high heat. Add the corn and cook it, stirring occasionally, for 4 to 5 minutes, until the corn is brown and beginning to char. Remove the corn from the heat and set it aside. Let the corn cool.

In a large bowl, combine the mayonnaise, yogurt, and lime juice and zest. Season the mixture with the salt and black pepper. Add the corn, avocado, coleslaw mix, cilantro, jalapeño, and green onion. Stir to combine. Taste the slaw and season it with salt and black pepper as needed. Top the slaw with the queso fresco cheese. Set the slaw aside while you make the tacos.

To make the tacos, press the blackening seasoning into the cod. Heat the oil in a medium heavy-bottomed skillet over medium-high heat. Add the cod and cook it for 3 to 4 minutes, until the blackening seasoning darkens and becomes almost black. Flip the fish and cook it 3 to 4 minutes, until it is cooked through and easily flakes with a fork.

Serve the fish in the tortillas topped with the Mexican corn slaw.

Picky Eaters: *If you are sensitive to spice, you may want to make these tacos with salmon instead of cod. The sweeter flesh of the salmon tones down the spice in the blackening seasoning. Sometimes we make a fish-stick option for the kids as well. They will top their crispy tacos with cabbage, avocado, and lime juice and eat plain corn on the side.*

Shortcut Refried Beans (N)

It's hard to beat homemade refried beans, but they take forever. Instead of settling for a premade option in a can, make these semi-homemade refried beans that taste almost as good as the real thing.

Serves: 2

Total Time: 20 minutes

1 tsp olive oil

¼ cup (36 g) diced onion

1 clove garlic, minced

1 cup (169 g) canned pinto beans, drained and rinsed

⅓ to ½ cup (80 to 120 ml) chicken broth

Salt, as needed

Black pepper, as needed

¼ cup (62 g) pico de gallo

2 tbsp (16 g) shredded Cheddar cheese

Heat the oil in a medium skillet over medium heat. Add the onion and garlic. Cook them for 4 to 5 minutes, until the onion begins to soften. Add the pinto beans and broth. Cook the beans for about 5 minutes, until they are warm. Turn off the heat and season the beans with the salt and black pepper.

Mash the beans using a potato masher or wooden spoon.

Top the beans with the pico de gallo and Cheddar cheese. Cover the skillet for 2 to 3 minutes, until the Cheddar cheese melts.

Recipe Ideas: *There are so many ways to customize refried beans. Make them spicy by adding a diced jalapeño with the onion. Add smokiness with a pinch of cumin or canned chipotle pepper in adobo. Use black beans instead of pinto for a different twist.*

Chickpea Pizza (O)

You will immediately fall in love with this nutty, crispy chickpea crust that packs more fiber, protein, and nutrients that a standard pizza dough. It's also a great plant-based source of iron. Add all of your favorite toppings for a healthier spin on family pizza night.

Serves: 2

Total Time: 50 minutes

1 cup (130 g) chickpea flour

1 cup (240 ml) warm water

2 tbsp (30 ml) olive oil, divided

½ tsp garlic powder

½ tsp Italian seasoning

Salt, as needed

Black pepper, as needed

½ cup (120 ml) spaghetti sauce

⅔ cup (75 g) shredded part-skim mozzarella cheese

½ to 1 cup pizza toppings of choice

In a medium bowl, mix together the chickpea flour, warm water, 1 tablespoon (15 ml) of the oil, garlic powder, Italian seasoning, salt, and black pepper until the ingredients are well combined. Let the mixture rest for at least 30 minutes.

Preheat the oven to 450°F (232°C).

Heat a 10- to 12-inch (25- to 30-cm) cast-iron skillet over medium-high heat. After 2 to 3 minutes, once the skillet is very hot, add the remaining 1 tablespoon (15 ml) of oil and swirl the skillet around to coat the skillet with the oil. You may also want to spray the skillet with cooking spray if things tend to stick to it. Add the chickpea mixture and swirl it around the skillet. It will bubble on the edges. Place the skillet in the oven and cook the pizza crust for 15 minutes, until it is firm.

Remove the skillet from the oven and spread the pizza crust with the spaghetti sauce. Add the mozzarella cheese and pizza toppings. Return the pizza to the oven for 5 minutes, until the cheese is melted. Remove the pizza from the oven and let it rest for 5 minutes before serving.

Picky Eaters: *Although I highly recommend you give this pizza a try, you can also pick up a store-bought pizza dough (ideally whole-wheat) and make your own pizza at home. Try to include some veggies in the toppings.*

Simply Yogurt Caesar Salad (P)

My whole family will happily eat Caesar salad, but all I can think about is the fact that they are eating more mayonnaise-based dressing, bread, and cheese than salad. This lightened-up version, made with Greek yogurt, tastes just as good and is actually good for you.

Serves: 2

Total Time: 20 minutes

1 small sourdough roll

Salt, as needed

Black pepper, as needed

3 tbsp (48 g) nonfat Greek yogurt

2 tbsp (10 g) shredded Parmesan cheese

1 tbsp (15 ml) fresh lemon juice

½ tbsp (8 ml) olive oil

1 tsp Worcestershire sauce

½ clove garlic, minced

¼ tsp anchovy paste (optional)

3 cups (225 g) coarsely chopped romaine lettuce

Preheat the oven or toaster oven to 400°F (204°C). Spray a large baking sheet with cooking spray.

Chop the sourdough roll into cubes and place them onto the prepared baking sheet. Spray them with cooking spray. Season them with the salt and black pepper. Bake the bread cubes for 8 to 10 minutes, until they are crispy. Remove them from the oven and set them aside.

In a small bowl, mix together the yogurt, Parmesan cheese, lemon juice, oil, Worcestershire sauce, garlic, and anchovy paste (if using). Add a splash of water if the mixture is too thick. Season the dressing with black pepper. If possible, let the dressing rest in the fridge for 30 minutes to allow the flavors to deepen.

Place the romaine lettuce in a salad bowl. Add the dressing and toss with lettuce to coat it in the dressing. Add the croutons and serve.

Know Your Ingredients: *Anchovy paste sounds like an intimidating ingredient, but it's one that can impart tons of umami flavor to any dish. It basically tastes salty and savory without a strong fish flavor. Give it a shot. Soon you will be using it for pasta, soups, and marinades.*

Week 4

We are in the homestretch as we enter the fourth week of meal planning together, but I hope this is just the start of your meal planning journey. More importantly, I hope you are falling in love with mealtime again and feel stronger and healthier. As we jump into the final week, take a minute to write any wins you have experienced along the way—big or small—and celebrate them! Use them as motivation to stay aboard the meal planning train.

Weekly Calendar

	Breakfast	Lunch	Dinner
Sunday	Pesto and Cherry Tomato Frittata (A, page 145) *with whole-wheat toast*	Cheesy Broccoli and Cauliflower Chowder (D, page 150)	Slow Cooker Citrus Carnitas with Pineapple Salsa (E, page 153) *with Cowboy Caviar (F, page 154) and corn tortillas*
Monday	Apple-Cinnamon Granola (B, page 146) *with ½ cup (125 g) yogurt and fresh fruit*	Slow Cooker Citrus Carnitas with Pineapple Salsa* (E, page 153) *with Cowboy Caviar (F, page 154) and 1 cup (30 g) greens*	One-Pot American Chop Suey (G, page 157)
Tuesday	Pesto and Cherry Tomato Frittata* (A, page 145) *with whole-wheat toast*	Cheesy Broccoli and Cauliflower Chowder* (D, page 150)	Crispy Coconut Chicken Strips (H, page 158) *with Sesame-Mandarin Green Beans (I, page 161)*
Wednesday	Apple-Cinnamon Granola* (B, page 146) *with ½ cup (125 g) yogurt and fresh fruit*	Slow Cooker Citrus Carnitas with Pineapple Salsa* (E, page 153) *with ½ cup (30 g) canned black beans and 1 cup (30 g) greens*	Asian Peanut Lettuce Wraps (J, page 162) *with ½ cup (80 g) cooked brown rice*
Thursday	Pesto and Cherry Tomato Frittata* (A, page 145) *with whole-wheat toast*	Crispy Coconut Chicken Strips* (H, page 158) *with 1 cup (30 g) greens*	Sweet and Spicy Pepper Jelly Chicken and Cauliflower (K, page 165) *with ½ cup (80 g) cooked couscous*
Friday	Apple-Cinnamon Granola* (B, page 146) *with ½ cup (125 g) yogurt and fresh fruit*	Asian Peanut Lettuce Wraps* (J, page 162) *with ½ cup (59 g) shelled edamame*	Shrimp Scampi Cakes (L, page 166) *with Crispy Garlic Squash Fries (M, page 169)*
Saturday	Blueberry-Maple Breakfast Sausage (C, page 149) *with 2 fried eggs and fresh fruit*	Shrimp Scampi Cakes* (L, page 166) *with ½ cup (80 g) cooked brown rice and 1 cup (30 g) greens*	Sloppy Joe–Stuffed Sweet Potatoes (N, page 170) *with green salad*

* Indicates leftovers

Shopping List

Dairy and Refrigerated Items

- ¼ cup (60 ml) skim milk (A)
- ½ cup (56 g) shredded part-skim mozzarella cheese (A)
- 16 eggs (A, C, H, L, M)
- 3 cups (750 g) flavored Greek yogurt (B)
- ½ cup (120 ml) 2% milk (D)
- 1 cup (120 g) shredded Cheddar cheese (D, N)
- ⅓ cup (80 ml) orange juice (E)
- 1½ tbsp (8 g) shredded Parmesan cheese (M)

Produce

- 2 cups (300 g) cherry tomatoes (A, F)
- Fresh fruit for breakfast (B, C)
- ⅓ cup (33 g) fresh blueberries (C)
- 12 cloves garlic (D, E, G, J, L, N)
- 1¼ yellow onions (D, G, N)
- 3 carrots (D, J, N)
- 2 ribs celery (D, N)
- 2 cups (330 g) pineapple (E)
- 1 jalapeño (E)
- 3 red bell peppers (E, F, G)
- 8 cups (240 g) greens (E, F, H, L)
- 7 limes (E, F, J)
- ¾ cup (26 g) cilantro (E, F, J, K)
- 1 red onion (E, F, K)
- 1 avocado (F)
- 1 green bell pepper (G, N)
- 8 oz (224 g) green beans (I)
- ½ mandarin orange (I)
- 2 tsp (2 g) ginger (J)
- 1 cup (75 g) mushrooms (J)
- 1 head butter lettuce (J)
- 5 green onions (J, N)
- 2 cups (460 g) cauliflower florets (K)
- 1½ lemons (L)
- 4 cups (120 g) arugula (L)
- 1 tomato (L)
- 3 tbsp (9 g) parsley (L, N)
- 1 summer squash (M)
- 2 sweet potatoes (N)
- Green salad for one meal (N)

Meat, Poultry, and Fish

- 1½ lb (675 g) 93% lean ground turkey (C, J)
- 2 lb (900 g) lean pork shoulder (E)
- 8 oz (224 g) 90% lean ground beef (G)
- 1⅓ lb (600 g) boneless, skinless chicken breast (H)
- 10 oz (280 g) boneless, skinless chicken thighs (K)
- 1 lb (450 g) raw frozen shrimp, peeled and deveined (L)

Grains, Pasta, and Bulk Items

- 2 cups (160 g) old-fashioned oats (B)
- ½ cup (55 g) sliced almonds (B)
- ½ cup (55 g) cashews (B)
- 2 tbsp (20 g) chia seeds (B)
- ¾ cup (68 g) dried apples (B)
- 2 cups (280 g) cellentani pasta (G)
- 2 cups (320 g) cooked brown rice (J, L)
- 1 cup (160 g) cooked couscous (K)
- ½ cup (101 g) green lentils (N)

Packaged, Canned, and Jarred Items

- 3 tbsp (48 g) pesto (A)
- Whole-wheat bread (A)
- ¼ cup (62 g) unsweetened applesauce (B)
- 2 cups (480 ml) low-sodium chicken broth (D)
- ¾ cup (98 g) canned cannellini beans (D)
- 4 corn tortillas (E)
- 24 oz (680 g) canned black beans (F)
- 15 oz (420 g) canned black-eyed peas (F)
- 8 oz (224 g) canned corn (F)
- 1 cup (240 g) low-sodium beef broth (G)
- ¾ cup (169 g) canned fire-roasted tomatoes (G)

(Continued)

Shopping List (Continued)

- 1 tbsp (14 g) tomato paste (G)
- 1½ cups (360 ml) tomato sauce (G, N)
- 3 tbsp (33 g) peanut butter (J)
- 1 cup (118 g) shelled edamame (J)
- 2 tbsp (40 g) hot pepper jelly (K)
- 2 tbsp (40 g) apricot preserves (K)

Pantry Spices

- Pure vanilla extract (B)
- Ground cinnamon (B)
- Dried sage (C)
- Smoked paprika (C)
- Onion powder (C)
- Garlic powder (C, F, H, M)
- Ground nutmeg (D)
- 2 dried bay leaves (D, G)

- Dried oregano (E)
- Ground cumin (E, F, N)
- Paprika (E, N)
- Red pepper flakes (G)
- Italian seasoning (G, M)
- Chili powder (N)

Refrigerated Items

- Butter (D, L)
- Worcestershire sauce (G, N)
- Asian garlic chili paste (I)
- Low-sodium soy sauce (J)
- Dijon mustard (N)

Other Items

- Coconut oil (B)
- Pure maple syrup (B, C)

- Olive oil (C, F, G, K, L, N)
- 2 cups (460 g) frozen cauliflower (D)
- 3 cups (525 g) frozen broccoli (D)
- White whole-wheat flour (D)
- Honey (F, J, N)
- ½ cup (40 g) unsweetened shredded coconut (H)
- Brown sugar (H)
- 1 cup (55 g) panko breadcrumbs (H, L)
- ½ tbsp (5 g) sesame seeds (I)
- Sesame oil (I, J)
- 2 tbsp (20 g) peanuts (J)
- 3 tbsp (18 g) seasoned breadcrumbs (M)
- Cooking spray

Game Plan

Now that you have hit a rhythm, you know what you need. Check your schedule, decide what needs to be prepped and what may need a kitchen hack. Let's finish strong.

Meal Prep

- Prepare the Apple-Cinnamon Granola (B, page 146).

- Make and freeze the Blueberry-Maple Breakfast Sausage (C, page 149).

- Make the dressing for the Cowboy Caviar (F, page 154).

- Make the sauce for the One-Pot American Chop Suey (G, page 157). Bring it to a boil before adding the pasta.

- Make the sauce for the Asian Peanut Lettuce Wraps (J, page 162), or prep the whole meal.

- Make brown rice for dinner (J, page 162) and lunch (L, page 166).

- Make the sloppy joe filling and bake the sweet potatoes (N, page 170).

- Optionally, prep the produce like so:

  - **Onion:** 1 yellow onion, diced (D, page 150; G, page 157)

  - **Carrot:** ½ carrot, finely chopped (D, page 150); ¼ cup (32 g), diced (N, page 170)

  - **Celery:** ½ rib, finely chopped (D, page 150); ¼ cup (56 g), diced (N, page 170)

  - **Pineapple:** 2 cups (330 g), diced (E, page 153)

  - **Red bell peppers:** 2 peppers, diced (E, page 153; F, page 154)

  - **Red onion:** ½ cup (72 g), diced (E, page 153; F, page 154)

  - **Green bell pepper:** 1 pepper, diced (G, page 157; N, page 170)

  - **Green beans:** 8 oz (224 g), trimmed (I, page 161)

  - **Cauliflower:** 2 cups (460 g) florets (K, page 165)

  - Prep fruit for breakfasts

  - Measure out greens, black beans, and edamame for lunches

- Freeze the chicken thighs if needed.

Daily Tips

- **Sunday:** Start the Slow Cooker Citrus Carnitas (E, page 153) at least 8 hours before dinner.

- **Wednesday:** Place the chicken thighs in the fridge to defrost if necessary.

- **Thursday:** Couscous only takes 5 minutes to prepare, so make it while the chicken cooks.

- **Friday:** Start with the Crispy Garlic Squash Fries (M, page 169). You can prep and cook the Shrimp Scampi Cakes (L, page 166) while they cook.

Kitchen Hacks

- **Sunday:** For a leaner and quicker cooking option, use pork tenderloin. It will cook in 3 to 4 hours but won't be nearly as tender. By precut pineapple to save time on the salsa.

- **Monday:** Instead of making your own sauce, simply cook the onions, peppers, garlic, and beef. Add a jar of your favorite spaghetti sauce. Cook the pasta on the side and toss everything together.

- **Wednesday:** Use store-bought peanut sauce instead of making your own.

- **Friday:** Grab a bag of frozen veggie fries instead of making your own.

- **Saturday:** Use canned lentils instead of cooking them from scratch. Just make sure to rinse them well.

Pesto and Cherry Tomato Frittata (A)

Pesto is a staple in our house to build flavor-packed dishes without a lot of work. It can be used for so much more than pasta. We love pairing it with eggs and fresh cherry tomatoes for an Italian-inspired frittata that's filled with flavor.

Serves: 6

Total Time: 35 minutes

8 eggs

¼ cup (60 ml) skim milk

3 tbsp (48 g) pesto

¾ tsp kosher salt

¼ tsp black pepper

1 cup (150 g) cherry tomatoes, quartered

½ cup (56 g) shredded part-skim mozzarella cheese, divided

Preheat the oven to 350°F (177°C). Spray an 8 x 8–inch (20 x 20–cm) baking dish with cooking spray.

In a medium bowl, whisk together the eggs, milk, pesto, salt, and black pepper.

Spread the cherry tomatoes and ¼ cup (28 g) of the mozzarella cheese in the bottom of the baking dish. Pour the eggs over the tomatoes and cheese. Sprinkle the remaining ¼ cup (28 g) of mozzarella cheese on top.

Bake the frittata for 23 to 28 minutes, until the eggs are puffed up and cooked. It's okay if the center jiggles slightly since the frittata will continue to cook as it cools. Let the frittata cool for at least 10 minutes before serving to allow it to set.

Recipe Ideas: *Once you start putting pesto in your eggs, you won't want to stop. Explore different combinations of proteins, veggies, and cheeses. A few of my favorites include pesto, goat cheese, and roasted red peppers; pesto, chickpeas, sun-dried tomatoes, and feta; or pesto, roasted broccoli, and sharp Cheddar cheese.*

Apple-Cinnamon Granola (B)

For a long time, I stayed away from granola since it is usually packed with oil and sugar. That all changed when I started using applesauce as a base. It sweetens the granola without tons of sugar and adds a delicious, subtle apple flavor.

Serves: 6

Total Time: 40 minutes

¼ cup (62 g) unsweetened applesauce

¼ cup (60 ml) pure maple syrup

2 tbsp (30 g) coconut oil

1 tsp pure vanilla extract

2 cups (160 g) old-fashioned oats

½ cup (55 g) sliced almonds

½ cup (55 g) cashews, coarsely chopped

2 tbsp (20 g) chia seeds

1 tsp ground cinnamon

½ tsp kosher salt

¾ cup (68 g) coarsely chopped dried apples

Preheat the oven to 350°F (177°C). Line a large baking sheet with parchment paper.

In a small saucepan over medium heat, combine the applesauce, maple syrup, coconut oil, and vanilla. Cook the mixture for 3 to 4 minutes, until it is combined and smooth.

In a large bowl, toss together the oats, almonds, cashews, chia seeds, cinnamon, and salt. Add the applesauce mixture and mix well. Spread the granola out in a single layer about ½ inch (1 cm) thick on the prepared baking sheet.

Bake the granola for 25 to 30 minutes, until it is light brown. Let it cool for at least 30 minutes for the granola to harden and become crispy. Break the granola into chunks, transfer it to a medium bowl, and toss it with the dried apples. Store the granola in an airtight container.

Recipe Blueprint: *Use this base recipe to make all kinds of granola. Add your favorite nuts, seeds, dried fruits, and sweet treats. Some of my favorite combinations include pepitas, dried cranberries, and white chocolate chips; or peanuts, sunflower seeds, and carob chips.*

Blueberry-Maple Breakfast Sausage (C)

Because I grew up in New England, blueberries and maple syrup are near and dear to my heart. They served as inspiration for these easy homemade breakfast sausages, which are sweet, savory, and so much healthier than store-bought breakfast sausages.

Serves: 2

Total Time: 20 minutes

8 oz (224 g) 93% lean ground turkey

⅓ cup (33 g) fresh blueberries

½ tbsp (8 ml) pure maple syrup

¼ tsp kosher salt

¼ tsp dried sage or thyme

¼ tsp smoked paprika

¼ tsp garlic powder

¼ tsp onion powder

⅛ tsp black pepper

½ tbsp (8 ml) olive oil

In a medium bowl, combine the turkey, blueberries, maple syrup, salt, sage, smoked paprika, garlic powder, onion powder, and black pepper. Use your hands to mix the ingredients together, being careful not to compress the meat too much. Shape the meat into patties, using ¼ cup (60 g) for each patty. Press each portion of meat into a thin, round patty.

Heat the oil in a medium skillet over medium heat. Add the sausage patties and cook them for 4 to 5 minutes per side, until they are brown and their internal temperature reaches 165°F (74°C).

Leftover Love: *These breakfast sausage patties freeze well and are great to grab for some extra protein at breakfast. Let them cool completely before freezing, and reheat them in a skillet or the microwave. They also make an amazing breakfast sandwich—healthy McGriddle, anyone?*

Cheesy Broccoli and Cauliflower Chowder (D)

After surveying lots of friends, I realized they wanted a creamy, cheesy soup without all the calories and fat. This chowder was my solution. The secret to making this soup creamy without mountains of cream is white beans. They add creaminess, fiber, and nutrients, and you won't even know they are there.

Serves: 4

Total Time: 40 minutes

½ tbsp (8 g) butter

½ yellow onion, diced

½ carrot, finely chopped

½ rib celery, finely chopped

1 to 2 cloves garlic, minced

1 tbsp (8 g) white whole-wheat flour

2 cups (480 ml) low-sodium chicken broth

½ cup (120 ml) 2% milk

2 cups (460 g) frozen cauliflower

3 cups (525 g) frozen broccoli

¾ cup (98 g) canned cannellini beans, drained and rinsed

¼ tsp kosher salt

Black pepper, as needed

Pinch of nutmeg (optional)

¾ cup (90 g) shredded Cheddar cheese, plus more as needed

Melt the butter in a large pot over medium-high heat. Add the onion, carrot, celery, and garlic. Cook the vegetables for 6 to 8 minutes, stirring often, until the onion is translucent and the other vegetables have softened. Add the flour and stir to coat the vegetables. Add the broth, milk, cauliflower, broccoli, cannellini beans, salt, black pepper, and nutmeg (if using).

Bring the soup to a simmer and cook it for 20 minutes, until the broccoli and cauliflower are very tender.

Add the Cheddar cheese, about ¼ cup (30 g) at a time, stirring it into the soup until the soup is smooth.

Add half of the soup to a blender. Blend until the soup is smooth. Return the blended soup to the pot. Season the soup with salt and black pepper if needed. Serve with extra Cheddar cheese if desired.

If You're Craving Crunch: *Make some easy croutons. Preheat the oven to 375°F (191°C). Slice or tear 6 slices of whole-grain bread into bite-size pieces. Toss them with 2 tablespoons (30 ml) of olive oil, ¾ teaspoon of garlic powder, ½ teaspoon of kosher salt, and black pepper as needed. Spread out the bread in a single layer on a medium baking sheet. Bake the croutons for 15 to 20 minutes, shaking the baking sheet halfway through the cooking time.*

Know Your Ingredients: *In a soup like this, cheese really matters. Since we are using about a third of the cheese used in a standard cheesy soup, make sure to choose a strong, pungent, delicious Cheddar. My favorite is extra-sharp aged Cheddar. Shred it yourself for a smoother soup.*

Slow Cooker Citrus Carnitas with Pineapple Salsa (E)

This simple pork taco recipe is inspired by two of my favorites: Mexican carnitas and Cuban mojo pork. It's garlicky, citrusy, and full of flavor. The pineapple salsa adds a light and refreshing touch.

Serves: 6

Total Time: 8 hours and 30 minutes

Pork

Olive oil, as needed (optional)

2 lb (900 g) lean pork shoulder, trimmed

¼ cup (60 ml) orange juice

¼ cup (60 ml) fresh lime juice

1 tsp ground cumin

1 tsp dried oregano

1 tsp kosher salt

¼ tsp black pepper

3 cloves garlic, minced

1 dried bay leaf

Pineapple Salsa

2 cups (330 g) diced fresh pineapple

1 red bell pepper, diced

1 jalapeño, diced

2 tbsp (6 g) finely chopped fresh cilantro

2 tbsp (18 g) diced red onion

1½ tbsp (23 ml) fresh lime juice

1½ tbsp (23 ml) orange juice

Salt, as needed

Black pepper, as needed

Make the pork. For the best flavor, heat a small amount of oil in a large heavy skillet over medium-high heat. Add the pork and sear it for 3 to 4 minutes on each side. If you don't have time, skip this step. Add the pork to a large slow cooker.

In a small bowl, mix together the orange juice, lime juice, cumin, oregano, salt, black pepper, and garlic. Pour this mixture over the pork. Add the bay leaf. Cook the pork on low for 8 hours.

Shred the pork with two forks and let it marinate in the cooking juices for 30 minutes to soak up the flavors.

Meanwhile, make the pineapple salsa. In a medium bowl, combine the pineapple, bell pepper, jalapeño, cilantro, onion, lime juice, orange juice, salt, and black pepper.

Serve the pork carnitas with the pineapple salsa.

Optional Step: *For crispy carnitas, remove the pork from the slow cooker with a slotted spoon and place it on a large baking sheet covered with foil. Broil the carnitas for 3 to 5 minutes, until they are brown and crispy.*

Recipe Ideas: *If you are missing spice in this dish, consider two quick options for kicking things up. Try adding 1 to 2 canned chipotle peppers to the pork while it cooks. This adds heat and some smokiness. Alternatively, add an extra jalapeño or swap it for a spicier pepper, like a serrano or habanero, in the pineapple salsa.*

Cowboy Caviar (F)

I am obsessed with this Southern spin on a classic bean salad. It maintains its southern roots with the black-eyed peas but is updated with fresh cilantro, avocado, and the tastiest honey-lime dressing. It also makes a great picnic or barbecue side.

Serves: 4

Total Time: 15 minutes

Salad

15 oz (420 g) canned black beans, drained and rinsed

15 oz (420 g) canned black-eyed peas, drained and rinsed

8 oz (224 g) canned corn, drained and rinsed

⅓ cup (48 g) diced red onion

1 red bell pepper, diced

1 cup (150 g) cherry tomatoes, finely chopped

1 avocado, finely chopped

⅓ cup (17 g) finely chopped fresh cilantro

Dressing

2 tbsp (30 ml) olive oil

Juice of 2 limes

Zest of 2 limes

2 tsp (10 ml) honey

1 tsp kosher salt, plus more as needed

½ tsp ground cumin

½ tsp garlic powder

½ tsp paprika

To make the salad, toss together the black beans, black-eyed peas, corn, onion, bell pepper, cherry tomatoes, avocado, and cilantro in a medium bowl.

To make the dressing, whisk together the oil, lime juice, lime zest, honey, salt, cumin, garlic powder, and paprika in a small bowl. Drizzle the dressing over the salad and toss to combine. Season the salad with additional salt if needed.

Leftover Love: *Bean salads are a great option for meal prep since they tend to stay fresher in the fridge than green salads. However, they keep best if you pack the dressing and avocado separately so that the salad doesn't get watery or mushy.*

One-Pot American Chop Suey (G)

In New England, it's American chop suey; in the Midwest, it's called goulash; and sometimes it's just called beef macaroni—but no matter what you call it, this classic ground beef, macaroni, and tomato dish is always a hit. This version, with a homemade tomato sauce, is warm, comforting, and flavorful. In New England it's typically finished with a mound of Cheddar cheese, which is optional.

Serves: 2

Total Time: 50 minutes

1 tsp olive oil

½ yellow onion, diced

½ green bell pepper, diced

½ red bell pepper, diced

2 cloves garlic, minced

½ tbsp (2 g) Italian seasoning

⅛ tsp red pepper flakes (optional)

8 oz (224 g) 90% lean ground beef

½ tsp salt

¼ tsp black pepper

1 cup (240 ml) low-sodium beef broth

¾ cup (169 g) canned fire-roasted diced tomatoes, undrained

¾ cup (180 ml) tomato sauce

1 tbsp (14 g) tomato paste

½ tbsp (8 ml) Worcestershire sauce

1 dried bay leaf

2 cups (280 g) cellentani pasta or elbow macaroni

Heat the oil in a large pot over medium-high heat. Add the onion, green bell pepper, and red bell pepper. Cook the vegetables for about 5 minutes, stirring frequently, until they have softened but not browned. Add the garlic, Italian seasoning, and red pepper flakes (if using). Cook the mixture for about 1 minute, stirring often, until the garlic is fragrant. Add the beef and cook the mixture for 5 to 7 minutes, until the beef is brown.

Season the beef with the salt and black pepper. Add the broth, tomatoes, tomato sauce, tomato paste, Worcestershire sauce, and bay leaf. Reduce the heat to medium-low and simmer the beef mixture for 20 minutes.

Add the cellentani pasta and cook it for 12 to 15 minutes, until the pasta is cooked to your liking. Discard the bay leaf, then taste and season the American chop suey as needed before serving.

Kitchen Hack: *Don't have time to make homemade sauce? Try this instead: Get the pasta started. Meanwhile, brown the ground beef with ½ onion, 1 diced bell pepper, and a few cloves of minced garlic. Add a jar of your favorite spaghetti sauce, a splash of Worcestershire sauce, and a sprinkling of Italian seasoning. Season the mixture with salt and black pepper, and dinner is done.*

Crispy Coconut Chicken Strips (H)

If there is one meal in this cookbook that my kids could happily eat every single night, it's this one. They love the crunch and slight sweetness of the coconut, and I love that they are enjoying healthy baked chicken tenders with good-for-you ingredients.

Serves: 4

Total Time: 30 minutes

1⅓ lb (600 g) boneless, skinless chicken breasts, cut into 16 strips

Salt, as needed

Black pepper, as needed

½ cup (28 g) panko breadcrumbs

½ cup (40 g) unsweetened shredded coconut

1 tbsp (9 g) brown sugar

1 tsp garlic powder

2 eggs, beaten

Preheat the oven to 400°F (204°C). Spray a large baking sheet with cooking spray.

Season the chicken strips with the salt and black pepper. On a plate, mix together the panko breadcrumbs, coconut, brown sugar, and garlic powder. Place the eggs in a shallow dish next to the plate of breadcrumbs. Dip each chicken strip into the eggs and let the excess drip off. Then dredge the chicken strip in the coconut breadcrumbs. Place each chicken strip on the prepared baking sheet.

Spray the top of the chicken strips with cooking spray. Bake the chicken strips for 7 to 8 minutes per side, until they are light brown and their internal temperature reaches 165°F (74°C).

Leftover Love: *Once you see how quickly these get eaten, you will want extra in the freezer. Let the chicken tenders fully cool after they're cooked. Place them on a large baking sheet and freeze them for 3 to 4 hours, until they are frozen solid on the outside. Add them to a freezer-safe bag or container and store them in the freezer for 3 to 4 months. Reheat them in an oven preheated to 400°F (204°C) for 10 to 15 minutes.*

Sesame-Mandarin Green Beans (I)

This simple 15-minute green bean recipe is elevated by the simple addition of mandarin orange juice. It brings out the sweetness of the green beans and pairs really well with the earthiness in the sesame oil and sesame seeds.

Serves: 2

Total Time: 15 minutes

8 oz (224 g) green beans, trimmed

2 tbsp (30 ml) water

1 tsp sesame oil

½ clove garlic, minced

Zest of ½ mandarin orange

Salt, as needed

Black pepper, as needed

Juice of ½ mandarin orange

½ tbsp (5 g) sesame seeds

Heat a medium skillet over medium-high heat. Add the green beans and water to the skillet. Bring the water to a boil and cook the green beans for 3 to 4 minutes, until they are bright green. Drain any excess water.

Add the oil, garlic, mandarin orange zest, salt, and black pepper. Stir and cook the green beans for 2 to 3 minutes, until the green beans are crisp-tender.

Drizzle the mandarin orange juice over the green beans, then sprinkle them with the sesame seeds.

Optional Addition: *Add mandarin orange slices to the green beans.*

Know Your Ingredients: *Green beans need a little prep work before they get cooked. Start by washing and drying the beans, then trim the stem end. Normally you don't need to remove the opposite end as well, but you can if it seems tough or fibrous.*

Asian Peanut Lettuce Wraps (J)

My kids get just as excited about lettuce wrap night as they do about taco night—all it takes is a little marketing. Luckily, these peanut lettuce wraps don't need much selling. The creamy, savory, and sweet peanut sauce is enough to get everyone excited about dinner.

Serves: 4

Total Time: 20 minutes

2 tsp (10 ml) sesame oil

2 cloves garlic, minced

2 tsp (2 g) minced fresh ginger

1 lb (450 g) 93% lean ground turkey

1 cup (75 g) diced mushrooms

¼ cup (60 ml) low-sodium soy sauce

3 tbsp (33 g) peanut butter

2 tbsp (30 ml) hot water

1 tbsp (15 ml) fresh lime juice, plus more as needed

1 tbsp (15 ml) honey

1 tsp Asian garlic chili paste (optional)

Leaves of 1 head butter lettuce

1 cup (50 g) shredded carrots

¼ cup (13 g) finely chopped green onions

¼ cup (13 g) finely chopped fresh cilantro

2 tbsp (20 g) finely chopped peanuts

1 lime, cut into wedges

Heat the oil in a large skillet over medium-high heat. Add the garlic and ginger and cook it for 30 seconds, until it is fragrant. Add the turkey and mushrooms and cook them for 6 to 8 minutes, breaking the turkey up as it cooks.

Meanwhile, in a small bowl, mix together the soy sauce, peanut butter, water, lime juice, honey, and Asian garlic chili paste (if using).

Once the turkey is no longer pink, add the peanut sauce to the skillet. Stir to coat the turkey in the sauce. Cook the turkey for 2 to 3 minutes, until the sauce thickens and coats the turkey.

Serve the turkey wrapped in the butter lettuce leaves and topped with the carrots, green onions, cilantro, peanuts, and lime wedges.

Recipe Ideas: *If you love this peanut sauce as much as we do, you'll want to use it for other meals. Toss it with shredded chicken, use it for Asian pasta dishes or stir-fries, drizzle it on salads, and use it as a dipping sauce for everything from baked chicken strips to spring rolls.*

Sweet and Spicy Pepper Jelly Chicken and Cauliflower (K)

This is one of those simple recipes that will make people think you are an amazing cook. The combination of apricot preserves with hot pepper jelly and cilantro creates something special without lots of work.

Serves: 2

Total Time: 20 minutes

Cauliflower

2 cups (460 g) cauliflower florets

½ red onion, thinly sliced

2 tsp (10 ml) olive oil

Salt, as needed

Black pepper, as needed

Chicken

2 tbsp (40 g) hot pepper jelly

2 tbsp (40 g) apricot preserves

1 garlic clove, minced

¼ tsp salt

¼ tsp black pepper

10 oz (280 g) boneless, skinless chicken thighs

⅛ cup (6 g) finely chopped fresh cilantro (optional)

Preheat the oven to 400°F (204°C).

To make the cauliflower, toss the cauliflower and onion with the oil in a medium bowl. Season the cauliflower and onion liberally with salt and black pepper. Spread out the vegetables in a single layer on a large baking sheet. Roast them for 15 minutes.

Meanwhile, make the chicken. In a large bowl, combine the hot pepper jelly, apricot preserves, garlic, salt, and black pepper. Add the chicken thighs to this mixture and let them marinate while the cauliflower cooks.

Remove the baking sheet from the oven. Nestle the chicken thighs among the cauliflower and onion. Top the chicken with any remaining marinade. Roast the mixture for 15 minutes, or until the chicken is cooked through and its juices run clear. Sprinkle the cilantro on top (if using) and serve.

Serving Suggestion: *If you are serving this meal with couscous, rice, or another grain, pour the pan juices over the grains for tons of extra flavor.*

Make It Yours: *This simple sauce works with many combinations of proteins and vegetables. Try making it with pork chops and green beans. Use it as a marinade for chicken drumsticks. It even tastes great spread on some salmon and baked in the oven. If spice doesn't work in your home, use all apricot preserves and add 1 to 2 tablespoons (15 to 30 ml) of soy sauce to cut the sweetness.*

Shrimp Scampi Cakes (L)

This dish delivers all the flavors of shrimp scampi packed into delicious shrimp cakes. Use these to make the most amazing seafood sliders, a special-occasion burger, an amazing addition to salad, or an appetizer everyone will go crazy for.

Serves: 4

Total Time: 25 minutes

1 lb (450 g) raw frozen shrimp, peeled and deveined, divided

2 cloves garlic

2 tbsp (8 g) fresh parsley

½ cup (28 g) panko breadcrumbs

1 egg

Zest of ½ lemon

Juice of 1½ lemons, divided

1 tsp kosher salt, plus more as needed

½ tsp black pepper, plus more as needed

1 tbsp (15 g) butter

4 cups (120 g) arugula

1 tomato, coarsely chopped

2 tsp (10 ml) olive oil

Add 8 ounces (224 g) of the shrimp, the garlic, and the parsley to a food processor. Pulse to create a chunky paste. Coarsely chop the remaining 8 ounces (224 g) of shrimp. Transfer the chopped and pulsed shrimp to a large bowl. Add the breadcrumbs, egg, lemon zest, juice of ½ lemon, salt, and black pepper. Mix until the ingredients are just combined. Using a ¼-cup (60-g) measuring cup, form the mixture into round patties.

Heat the butter in a medium skillet over medium-high heat. Working in batches if necessary, add the shrimp patties to the skillet and cook them for 3 to 4 minutes per side, until they are cooked through and brown.

In a medium bowl, toss together the arugula, tomato, oil, remaining lemon juice, additional salt, and additional black pepper. Serve the arugula alongside the shrimp patties.

Picky Eaters: *If shrimp isn't popular in your home, make these with fish instead. Follow the same instructions, adding your favorite whitefish, salmon, or even tuna instead of the shrimp.*

Crispy Garlic Squash Fries (M)

Everyone cooks with zucchini, but how often are you making summer squash? This delicately flavored veggie makes tasty fries when coated with breadcrumbs and Parmesan cheese. Serve them instead of potatoes for a healthier side.

Serves: 2

Total Time: 45 minutes

1 summer squash

Salt, as needed

3 tbsp (18 g) seasoned breadcrumbs

1½ tbsp (8 g) shredded Parmesan cheese

½ tsp garlic powder

¼ tsp Italian seasoning

Black pepper, as needed

1 egg white, whisked

Preheat the oven to 425°F (218°C). Spray a large baking sheet with cooking spray.

Cut the squash in half lengthwise, then each half into quarters. Cut those quarters in half. You should get 16 fries per squash.

Transfer the fries to a large bowl. Sprinkle the fries with salt and let them sit for 10 to 15 minutes. This draws out the water and helps the fries get extra crispy.

In another large bowl or plastic storage bag, mix together the breadcrumbs, Parmesan cheese, garlic powder, Italian seasoning, and black pepper.

Add the egg white to the squash and toss to coat the fries in the egg white. Add the fries to the breadcrumb mixture and gently toss to coat the fries in the breadcrumbs. Place the fries on the prepared baking sheet in a single layer. Spray the top of the fries with cooking spray.

Bake the fries for 20 to 22 minutes, flipping them halfway through the cooking time, until they are tender on the inside and crispy on the outside.

Recipe Blueprint: *Use this basic recipe to make all kinds of veggie fries. Use zucchini, green beans, asparagus, carrots, turnips, or even jicama. Change up the spices and replace the Parmesan with extra breadcrumbs depending on the flavor you want.*

Sloppy Joe–Stuffed Sweet Potatoes (N)

As I introduce more meatless main dishes into our diet, I love using something that's familiar, like these sloppy joes. By swapping out the meat with lentils and then stuffing everything into sweet potatoes, it becomes a hearty, nutritious dish everyone is excited to eat.

Serves: 2

Total Time: 40 minutes

½ cup (101 g) green lentils, rinsed and drained

1 cup (240 ml) water

2 sweet potatoes

½ tbsp (8 ml) olive oil

¼ onion, diced

¼ green bell pepper, diced

¼ cup (32 g) diced carrots

¼ cup (56 g) diced celery

1 clove garlic, minced

¾ cup (180 ml) tomato sauce

2 tsp (10 ml) honey, plus more as needed

½ tbsp (8 g) Dijon mustard

½ tbsp (8 ml) Worcestershire sauce

½ tsp chili powder, plus more as needed

¼ tsp paprika

⅛ tsp ground cumin

¼ cup (30 g) shredded Cheddar cheese

2 tbsp (6 g) thinly sliced green onions

1 tbsp (3 g) finely chopped fresh parsley

In a medium pot over medium-high heat, combine the lentils and water. Bring the lentils to a boil, then reduce the heat to low. Cook the lentils for 18 to 22 minutes, until they are tender. Drain any excess liquid.

Meanwhile, pierce the sweet potatoes all over with a fork. Microwave the sweet potatoes, uncovered, on high for 10 to 13 minutes, or until they are tender, turning them twice during the cooking time.

Heat the oil in a medium skillet over medium-high heat. Add the onion, bell pepper, carrots, and celery. Cook the vegetables for 6 to 8 minutes, until the vegetables begin to soften. Add the garlic and cook the mixture for 30 seconds, until the garlic is fragrant. Add the tomato sauce, honey, mustard, Worcestershire sauce, chili powder, paprika, and cumin. Bring the mixture to a simmer and let it cook while the lentils finish cooking. Add the drained lentils to the sauce and stir well. Cook the sloppy joe mixture for 3 to 4 minutes to allow the sauce to thicken. Taste the lentils and add more honey if needed.

Carefully slice open the sweet potatoes. Add the lentil sloppy joes and top the stuffed sweet potatoes with the Cheddar cheese, green onions, and parsley.

Picky Eaters: *If lentils are a stopping point, you can make this recipe with a more traditional sloppy joe protein, like ground beef, ground turkey, or ground chicken. Simply brown the meat and add it right into the sauce. For an alternative vegetarian option, consider chickpeas or pinto beans.*

Bonus Recipes

The recipes in this section have two purposes. First, they can serve as options when you need to swap in a different recipe if there is something that won't work for your family or schedule. Additionally, during week 5 and beyond, you will be building your own meal plans. Use a combination of these bonus recipes and your favorites from the first four weeks to build your week 5 meal plan.

Fancy Toast Five Ways

If I had to pick one food to eat forever, it might just be really good bread and butter. Unfortunately, since that combination is almost nutritionally void, I opt to make fancy toast a regular in my morning rotation. Following are some of my favorites. All of them start hearty with whole-grain sprouted toast. Each combination is packed with whole grains, protein, and healthy fats to keep you full all morning.

Serves: 1

Coconut PB&J

Peanut or almond butter

Sliced strawberries or raspberries

Sprinkle of chia seeds

Dollop of coconut yogurt

Lox and Cream Cheese

Veggie cream cheese

Sliced cucumber

Sliced tomato

Sliced red onion

Smoked salmon

Fresh dill

Open Faced BTLA

Smashed avocado

Everything bagel seasoning

Crispy turkey bacon

Sliced tomato

Sprouts

Fried egg (optional)

Three-Year-Old Special

Cream cheese

Sliced strawberries

Sliced banana

Hemp seeds

Drizzle of honey

Drizzle of runny almond butter

The Elvis

Peanut butter

Bananas

Crispy turkey bacon

Drizzle of pure maple syrup

Toast your favorite whole grain bread. Add a thin layer of spread and pile on the toppings.

Recipe Idea: *All of these can be made with sweet potato toast. Carefully slice the sweet potato into ¼-inch (6-mm)-thick pieces. You can peel the sweet potato first or leave the skin on. Place the sweet potato in the toaster on the high setting. Toast the sweet potato through 2 to 3 cycles, until the sweet potato is cooked through and crisp on the outside.*

Creamy Chocolate Smoothie

This magical smoothie tastes kind of like a chocolate shake. Not exactly, but it's close. The tofu adds creaminess and protein. The oats add whole grains and fiber. Plus, all the sweetness comes from a very ripe banana, so it's a treat that isn't packed with sugar.

Serves: 2

Total Time: 5 minutes

1 very ripe banana

⅓ cup (10 g) baby spinach

¼ cup (62 g) silken tofu

¼ cup (20 g) old-fashioned oats

2 tbsp (14 g) unsweetened cocoa powder

1 tbsp (11 g) nut butter

1½ cups (360 ml) unsweetened almond milk

½ cup (350 g) ice cubes

Honey or pure maple syrup, as needed (optional)

In a blender, combine the banana, spinach, tofu, oats, cocoa powder, nut butter, milk, ice cubes, and honey (if using). Blend until the ingredients are smooth and creamy.

Leftover Love: *Turn leftovers into popsicles or smoothie bites by freezing your extra smoothie in your favorite silicone cookie or candy molds. This trick also works with fruit—anytime your kids don't finish their fruit, don't throw it out. Store it in a smoothie bag in the freezer, and you won't stress about wasting food.*

Italian Baked Eggs

This dish is one that I love to make on cold weekend mornings. It fills the house with the most amazing aroma and feels like a fancy brunch. Serve it with crusty bread or over some sautéed zucchini noodles for a healthier option.

Serves: 4

Total Time: 20 minutes

1 tbsp (15 ml) olive oil

½ onion, diced

2 cloves garlic, minced

2 cups (480 ml) spaghetti sauce

¼ cup (60 ml) skim milk

8 eggs

Salt, as needed

Black pepper, as needed

¼ cup (28 g) shredded part-skim mozzarella cheese

¼ cup (20 g) shredded Parmesan cheese

¼ cup (15 g) fresh basil leaves, finely chopped

Preheat the oven to 425°F (218°C).

Heat the oil in a medium cast-iron skillet over medium heat. Add the onion and cook it for 4 to 5 minutes, until it is translucent. Add the garlic and cook the mixture for 30 seconds, until the garlic is fragrant. Add the spaghetti sauce and milk. Stir to combine. Bring the sauce to a simmer.

Use the back of a spoon to make a small indentation in the sauce for each egg. Break the eggs into the indentations. Season everything well with the salt and black pepper. Place the skillet in the oven and bake the eggs for 7 to 10 minutes, until the egg whites just begin to look set.

Sprinkle the mozzarella cheese and Parmesan cheese on top of the eggs and return them to the oven for 2 to 3 minutes, until the cheeses melt and the eggs are cooked to your liking. Top the eggs with the basil and serve.

Recipe Blueprint: *Once you start making this dish, you will realize there are many possibilities for baked eggs. Use green salsa instead of spaghetti sauce to take it in a Mexican direction. Use crushed tomatoes and Middle Eastern spices to create a more shakshuka-style dish. Add extra veggies, chickpeas, and cheeses.*

Build-Your-Own Chicken Salad

Chicken salad is one of those things I love having in the fridge for quick sandwiches, salads, and wraps. It always starts with leftover or rotisserie chicken—and then things get crazy. These are our five favorite combinations.

Serves: 4

Total Time: 20 minutes

Chicken Salad Base

¼ cup (63 g) nonfat Greek yogurt

3 tbsp (42 g) low-fat mayonnaise

½ tbsp (8 ml) fresh lemon juice

½ tsp onion powder

½ tsp salt

½ tsp black pepper

1½ cups (210 g) finely chopped cooked chicken breast

Classic Chicken Salad

½ cup (113 g) diced celery

½ tsp celery seed

Waldorf Chicken Salad

1 apple, diced

¾ cup (75 g) halved red grapes

¼ cup (56 g) finely chopped celery

2 tbsp (6 g) finely chopped green onions

2 tbsp (14 g) finely chopped walnuts

Curried Chicken Salad

1 tbsp (6 g) curry powder

1 tbsp (20 g) mango chutney

½ cup (50 g) halved red grapes

¼ cup (32 g) diced carrots

2 tbsp (6 g) finely chopped green onions

Buffalo Chicken Salad

2 tbsp (30 ml) Buffalo wing sauce

¼ cup (56 g) diced celery

¼ cup (32 g) diced carrots

¼ cup (38 g) crumbled blue cheese

Cranberry-Almond Chicken Salad

¼ cup (25 g) dried cranberries

¼ cup (28 g) sliced almonds

¼ cup (56 g) diced celery

1 tsp honey

1 tsp Dijon mustard

½ tsp poppy seeds

To make the chicken salad base, stir together the yogurt, mayonnaise, lemon juice, onion powder, salt, and black pepper in a large bowl. Fold in the chicken. Add any desired additions.

Leftover Love: *Assuming you are starting with relatively fresh chicken, chicken salad will last in the fridge for 4 to 5 days. With that said, I like to keep ingredients like grapes and nuts separate so that they maintain their crunch.*

Turkey Sausage and Tortellini Soup

On a cold night, this is exactly what I want to be eating. The spices of turkey sausage are the key to creating a flavorful broth without the need for lots of spices. Paired with plenty of veggies and cheesy stuffed spinach tortellini, this soup gets me ready for a family night in.

Serves: 6

Total Time: 45 minutes

1 tbsp (15 ml) olive oil

1 onion, diced

1 carrot, diced

1 rib celery, diced

1 lb (450 g) raw ground lean turkey sausage

4 cloves garlic, minced

2 tsp (2 g) Italian seasoning

1 dried bay leaf

4 cups (960 ml) chicken broth

1 (28-oz [784-g]) can crushed tomatoes

¼ cup (20 g) shredded Parmesan cheese

1 tsp salt

½ tsp black pepper

9 oz (525 g) fresh or dried spinach tortellini

4 cups (120 g) baby spinach

Heat the oil in a large pot over medium-high heat. Add the onion, carrot, and celery. Cook the vegetables for 4 to 5 minutes, until they begin to become translucent. Add the turkey sausage and brown it for 4 to 5 minutes, until it is cooked through and no longer pink. Add the garlic, Italian seasoning, and bay leaf. Cook the mixture for 30 to 60 seconds, until it is fragrant. Add the broth, tomatoes, Parmesan cheese, salt, and black pepper. Stir well.

Bring the soup to a simmer and cook it for 20 to 30 minutes.

Add the tortellini and spinach. If you are using fresh tortellini, cook the soup for 2 to 3 minutes. If you are using dried tortellini, cook the soup for 9 to 12 minutes. Taste and season the soup with salt and black pepper as needed. Discard the bay leaf before serving.

Recipe Ideas: *Swap out the sausage for plain ground turkey, chicken, or beef. Add a can of cannellini beans or chickpeas. Try swapping diced zucchini for the spinach. Use a different filled pasta. Make it creamy with the addition of some half-and-half.*

"Steak" and Cheese–Stuffed Zucchini

Now, this dish won't replace your favorite Philly cheesesteak, but it is a much healthier way to enjoy some of the same flavors. Using ground beef ensures the steak doesn't overcook in the oven and means you don't need to spend lots of time trying to slice it thinly.

Serves: 4

Total Time: 40 minutes

4 zucchini

2 tsp (10 ml) olive oil

½ onion, diced

½ green bell pepper, diced

1 cup (75 g) diced mushrooms

2 cloves garlic, minced

1 lb (450 g) 95% lean ground beef

1 cup (242 g) crushed tomatoes

1 tsp Italian seasoning

1 tsp Worcestershire sauce

Salt, as needed

Black pepper, as needed

½ cup (56 g) shredded provolone cheese

Preheat the oven to 400°F (204°C). Spray a medium baking dish with cooking spray.

Cut the zucchini in half lengthwise. Scoop out the zucchini centers using a spoon. Dice the flesh of zucchini to use in the filling. Place the hollowed zucchini in the prepared baking dish. Cover the baking dish with foil and bake the zucchini for 15 minutes, or until they are just beginning to soften.

Meanwhile, heat the oil in a large skillet over medium-high heat. Add the onion, bell pepper, mushrooms, and diced zucchini. Cook this mixture for 6 to 8 minutes, until the vegetables are tender. Add the garlic and cook the mixture for 30 seconds, until the garlic is fragrant. Add the beef, breaking it up as needed. Cook the filling for 6 to 8 minutes, until the beef is brown and cooked through. Add the tomatoes, Italian seasoning, and Worcestershire sauce. Taste the filling and season it with the salt and black pepper.

Fill each zucchini with the beef mixture and top each one with the provolone cheese. Bake the zucchini, uncovered, for 15 to 18 minutes, until they are fully cooked and the cheese has melted.

Kitchen Hack: *Instead of baking the zucchini to soften them, microwave the zucchini halves for 2 to 3 minutes, until they have softened.*

Slow Cooker Salsa Chicken Chili

We are huge pozole fans at our house, but it can be a labor of love. This pozole-inspired chicken chili uses salsa verde as the secret ingredient to add tons of flavor without the need for tons of ingredients. Use any combination of beans you like, and don't be scared to throw in some veggies.

Serves: 6

Total Time: 3 hours, 10 minutes

2 lb (900 g) boneless, skinless chicken thighs or breasts

2 tsp (4 g) ground cumin

1 tsp garlic powder

1 tsp onion powder

Salt, as needed

Black pepper, as needed

14 oz (392 g) canned pinto beans, drained and rinsed

14 oz (392 g) canned black beans, drained and rinsed

14 oz (392 g) canned hominy or corn, drained and rinsed

2 cups (480 ml) salsa verde

4 cups (906 ml) chicken broth

In a large slow cooker, combine the chicken thighs, cumin, garlic powder, onion powder, salt, black pepper, pinto beans, black beans, hominy, salsa verde, and broth. Stir to combine. Cook on low for 4 hours, or until the chicken's internal temperature reaches 165°F (74°C).

Remove the chicken from the slow cooker and either shred it or chop it finely. Return it to the slow cooker.

Serve the chili with your favorite chili toppings (such as shredded cheese, sour cream, avocado, baked tortilla chips, queso fresco cheese, diced onion, fresh cilantro, diced jalapeños, or fresh lime juice).

Know Your Ingredients: *The flavor in this chili is heavily dependent on the salsa verde, so make sure to choose one with lots of flavor. Don't be scared to reach for something spicy since the rest of the flavors in the soup will tame the spice.*

Baked Cilantro-Lime Salmon Packets

These easy salmon packets only take a few minutes to assemble and are one of my favorite dishes to serve guests. They are fun, flavorful, and always a hit.

Serves: 4

Total Time: 30 minutes

4 (5-oz [140-g]) salmon fillets

Salt, as needed

Black pepper, as needed

2 tbsp (30 g) butter, melted

2 tbsp (30 ml) honey

Juice of 2 limes

2 cloves garlic, minced

1 cup (250 g) canned corn, drained and rinsed

1 cup (60 g) canned black beans, drained and rinsed

1 cup (150 g) cherry tomatoes, halved

½ cup (88 g) diced green bell pepper

¼ cup (36 g) diced red onion

⅓ cup (17 g) finely chopped fresh cilantro

Preheat the oven to 400°F (204°C). Cut eight squares of foil measuring about 12 x 12 inches (30 x 30 cm). Layer two pieces of foil together to create 4 packets.

Season the salmon on both sides with the salt and black pepper.

In a small bowl, mix together the butter, honey, lime juice, and garlic. In a medium bowl, mix together the corn, black beans, cherry tomatoes, bell pepper, and onion.

Add about 1 cup (240 g) of the bean and corn mixture to each of the foil packets. Place a salmon fillet on top of each portion of the bean mixture. Pour the sauce over the salmon.

Close the packets and place them on a large baking sheet. Cook the packets for 10 minutes. Carefully open the packets. Increase the oven to broil and cook the salmon for 2 to 3 minutes to brown the top. Sprinkle the cilantro on top of each fillet and serve.

Kitchen Tip: *For best results, always let your salmon come to room temperature before cooking. Normally this takes between 15 and 20 minutes, but the extra time will ensure your salmon cooks evenly and correctly.*

Sheet-Pan Chicken and Vegetable Stir-Fry

This versatile recipe takes the standard stir-fry and makes it even easier to make by swapping out the skillet for a baking sheet. Serve it with some brown rice or quinoa for a healthy meal that's just as good as takeout.

Serves: 4

Total Time: 30 minutes

1⅓ lb (600 g) boneless, skinless chicken thighs, coarsely chopped

1 tbsp (15 ml) sesame oil

½ tsp black pepper

⅓ cup (80 ml) low-sodium soy sauce

⅓ cup (80 ml) water

2 tbsp (30 ml) hoisin sauce

2 tbsp (30 ml) honey

1 clove garlic, minced

1 tbsp (9 g) cornstarch

1 cup (175 g) small broccoli florets

1 cup (230 g) small cauliflower florets

1 cup (128 g) thinly sliced carrots

1 cup (160 g) snow peas

Preheat the oven to 400°F (204°C). Line a large baking sheet with foil and spray the foil with cooking spray.

Toss the chicken with the oil and black pepper on the prepared baking sheet. Spread out the chicken in a single layer on the prepared baking sheet. Bake the chicken for 10 minutes.

Meanwhile, combine the soy sauce, water, hoisin sauce, honey, garlic, and cornstarch in a small saucepan over medium-high heat. Bring the mixture to a boil, and then reduce the heat to low. Cook the sauce for 4 to 6 minutes, until it thickens and coats the back of a spoon, being careful not to burn it.

Remove the chicken from the oven. Add the broccoli, cauliflower, carrots, and snow peas to the baking sheet. Drizzle the mixture with the sauce and toss to coat. Cook the chicken and vegetables for 8 to 10 minutes, until the vegetables are crisp-tender.

Recipe Ideas: *Play around with the flavors in the stir-fry sauce to create different spins on this easy sheet-pan dinner. Add Sriracha for a spicy sauce, add ginger and lemongrass for extra punch, swap oyster or sweet chili sauce for the hoisin sauce, add some curry paste—you get the idea.*

Beyond the Book

I like to think about this book as meal planning bootcamp. My goal in providing you with these easy-to-follow meal plans is not only to make your life easier but also to convince you that meal planning needs to become part of your lifestyle.

My hope is that over the past four weeks, you not only have enjoyed amazing food but also that you have learned to love mealtime again. Sitting down to a meal should be something you look forward to. Eating together is fun—it nourishes our minds, bodies, and souls.

For most of humanity's history, family meals have been a staple of life for a reason. Family mealtime is a time to interact, to fill our engines, to find connection and meaning. Yet in the stress of everyday life, many of us lose that feeling of togetherness. I hope this book has helped you recapture it.

Now it's time to build that skill on your own.

For anyone beginning to meal plan on their own, my best advice is to embrace theme nights. Starting from a blank slate is tough. Checking off boxes is much easier, and it's actually what we have been doing for most of this book.

Here's a template to get you started. Fill it in with your own ideas and themes, always working to include a variety of proteins and cuisines.

Week 5

	Breakfast	Lunch	Dinner
Sunday	(egg dish)	(salad)	(slow cooker chicken)
Monday	(grains)	(dinner leftovers)	(pasta)
Tuesday	(leftover egg dish)	(salad leftovers)	(Asian turkey)
Wednesday	(leftover grains)	(dinner leftovers)	(sheet-pan beef)
Thursday	(leftover egg dish)	(dinner leftovers)	(family-favorite chicken)
Friday	(leftover grains)	(dinner leftovers)	(fish)
Saturday	(family favorite)	(dinner leftovers)	(tacos)

	Breakfast	Lunch	Dinner
Sunday	(egg dish)	(soup)	(slow cooker beef)
Monday	(grains)	(dinner leftovers)	(pasta)
Tuesday	(leftover egg dish)	(soup leftovers)	(Asian pork)
Wednesday	(leftover grains)	(dinner leftovers)	(sheet-pan chicken)
Thursday	(leftover egg dish)	(dinner leftovers)	(family-favorite turkey)
Friday	(leftover grains)	(dinner leftovers)	(shellfish)
Saturday	(family favorite)	(dinner leftovers)	(pizza)

Week 7

	Breakfast	Lunch	Dinner
Sunday	(egg dish)	(sandwich)	(slow cooker pork)
Monday	(grains)	(dinner leftovers)	(pasta)
Tuesday	(leftover egg dish)	(sandwich leftovers)	(Asian beef)
Wednesday	(leftover grains)	(dinner leftovers)	(sheet-pan chicken)
Thursday	(leftover egg dish)	(dinner leftovers)	(family-favorite chicken thighs)
Friday	(leftover grains)	(dinner leftovers)	(fish)
Saturday	(family favorite)	(dinner leftovers)	(burgers)

(Continued)

	Breakfast	Lunch	Dinner
Sunday	(egg dish)	(salad)	(slow cooker turkey)
Monday	(grains)	(dinner leftovers)	(pasta)
Tuesday	(leftover egg dish)	(salad)	(Asian chicken)
Wednesday	(leftover grains)	(dinner leftovers)	(sheet-pan pork)
Thursday	(leftover egg dish)	(dinner leftovers)	(family-favorite beef)
Friday	(leftover grains)	(dinner leftovers)	(shellfish)
Saturday	(family favorite)	(dinner leftovers)	(burritos)

Want more help? I provide weekly customizable meal plans, just like the ones in the book, on my website to keep the meal planning train moving. Visit https://www.slenderkitchen.com/meal-plans/.

If you want something more fluid, do some high-level thinking through proteins and themes. For example, you may want to include two meals with chicken, one with beef, one with pork, one with turkey, one with seafood, and one with vegetarian protein.

But most importantly, just start! Meal planning doesn't have to be hard.

Acknowledgments

To Joe, for being my number one taste tester and cheerleader. Thank you for always pushing me to accomplish more than I think is possible. Who would have imagined that our patio dreams on Beechwood would turn into this amazing business and journey? There is no one else I would want at my side.

To Noa and Charlie, for bringing so much joy, laughter, and love to our lives. It's hard to imagine our lives before you.

To Mom and Dad, for always encouraging me to pursue every single dream I've ever had. Your endless support and encouragement built a foundation to dream big.

To our friends and loved ones, who tasted recipes, tested recipes, and gave invaluable feedback and encouragement during this process. I couldn't have done this without your help, or our Fridays in the park.

To summer nights at the beach, where I learned just how much meals can build memories and deepen family connections. You are my people.

To Page Street for your belief in this book and support through the publishing process.

About the Author

Kristen McCaffrey is the home cook behind the popular recipe and meal planning website Slender Kitchen. With two busy little girls at home, Kristen is dedicated to making it easy to get healthy family meals on the table night after night.

Kristen became obsessed with meal planning after years of struggling to find the secret to making easy and affordable home-cooked meals. Between busy schedules, endless nights staring into the fridge wondering what was for dinner, and a struggle with weight loss, Kristen found meal planning to be the solution she was looking for. Now she wants to help others discover how meal planning can make life easier.

Kristen lives in Los Angeles, California, with her husband and two daughters, but she grew up in Massachusetts. Kristen attended the University of Notre Dame and has a master's degree from Loyola Marymount University.

Index

A

airtight containers, 22

almonds
Apple-Cinnamon Granola, 146
Cranberry-Almond Chicken Salad, 176
American Chop Suey, One-Pot, 157

apples
Apple-Cinnamon Granola, 146
Cheddar-Apple Chicken Burgers, 59
Cinnamon Apple and Pear Oatmeal, 109
Skillet Pork Tenderloin with Apples and Snap Peas, 89
Waldorf Chicken Salad, 176

artichokes: Creamy Spinach and Artichoke Pasta, 82

arugula: Shrimp Scampi Cakes, 166

asparagus
prepping, 25
Roasted Ranch Butternut Squash and Asparagus, 121

avocado
Cowboy Caviar, 154
Creamy Salsa Verde, 97
Open Faced BTLA, 173

B

bacon
Open Faced BTLA, 173
Sheet-Pan Sweet Potato and Veggie Breakfast Hash, 110
Turkey Bacon and Spinach Breakfast Sandwiches, 36

bananas
Blueberry-Banana Greek Yogurt Pancakes, 39
Creamy Chocolate Smoothie, 174
Three-Year-Old Special, 173
Zucchini Banana Bread Baked Oatmeal, 35

beans
Baked Cilantro-Lime Salmon Packets, 180
Cheesy Broccoli and Cauliflower Chowder, 150
Cilantro-Lime Cauliflower Rice and Beans, 86
Cowboy Caviar, 154
Crispy Baked Sweet Potato Taquitos, 97
Mini Meatloaves and Green Beans, 125
Sesame-Mandarin Green Beans, 161
Shortcut Refried Beans, 133
Skillet Turkey Enchiladas, 55
Slow Cooker Salsa Chicken Chili, 179

beef
Broiled Barbecue Flank Steak with Mango Salsa, 85
One-Pot American Chop Suey, 157
Slow Cooker Mediterranean Beef with Tzatziki, 43
"Steak" and Cheese–Stuffed Zucchini, 178

bell peppers. See peppers

black beans
Baked Cilantro-Lime Salmon Packets, 180
Cilantro-Lime Cauliflower Rice and Beans, 86
Cowboy Caviar, 154
Crispy Baked Sweet Potato Taquitos, 97
Slow Cooker Salsa Chicken Chili, 179

black-eyed peas: Cowboy Caviar, 154

blueberries
Blueberry-Banana Greek Yogurt Pancakes, 39
Blueberry-Maple Breakfast Sausage, 149

bread: Fancy Toast Five Ways, 173

breakfast, 18
Apple-Cinnamon Granola, 146
Blueberry-Banana Greek Yogurt Pancakes, 39
Blueberry-Maple Breakfast Sausage, 149
Cinnamon Apple and Pear Oatmeal, 109
Fancy Toast Five Ways, 173
Ham, Cheese, and Zucchini Breakfast Quesadillas, 107
Italian Baked Eggs, 175
Pepperoni Pizza Mini Frittatas, 69
Pesto and Cherry Tomato Frittata, 145
Pumpkin–Chocolate Chip Muffins, 70
Sheet-Pan Sweet Potato and Veggie Breakfast Hash, 110

Turkey Bacon and Spinach Breakfast Sandwiches, 36

Ultimate Breakfast Scramble, 73

Zucchini Banana Bread Baked Oatmeal, 35

broccoli

Cheesy Broccoli and Cauliflower Chowder, 150

Lemon-Garlic Roasted Broccoli and Polenta, 94

One-Pan Honey Mustard Salmon, Potatoes, and Broccoli, 56

prepping, 25

Sesame-Orange Chicken and Broccoli, 129

Sheet-Pan Chicken and Vegetable Stir-Fry, 181

Brussels sprouts

prepping, 25

Sheet-Pan Sweet Potato and Veggie Breakfast Hash, 110

Spicy Asian Brussels Sprouts, 81

bulk buying, 21

burgers

Cheddar-Apple Chicken Burgers, 59

Shrimp Scampi Cakes, 166

butternut squash

prepping, 25

Roasted Ranch Butternut Squash and Asparagus, 121

Slow Cooker Four-Veggie Lasagna, 114

C

cabbage, prepping, 25

cannellini beans: Cheesy Broccoli and Cauliflower Chowder, 150

carrots

Asian Peanut Lettuce Wraps, 162

Buffalo Chicken Salad, 176

Cashew Chicken and Pineapple Fried Rice, 48

Crunchy Thai Peanut and Mango Salad, 113

Curried Chicken Salad, 176

prepping, 25

Pumpkin–Chocolate Chip Muffins, 70

Sheet-Pan Chicken and Vegetable Stir-Fry, 181

Sloppy Joe–Stuffed Sweet Potatoes, 170

cashews

Apple-Cinnamon Granola, 146

Cashew Chicken and Pineapple Fried Rice, 48

cauliflower

Baked Pizza Pork Chops with Cauliflower, 51

Cheesy Broccoli and Cauliflower Chowder, 150

Cilantro-Lime Cauliflower Rice and Beans, 86

prepping, 25

Sheet-Pan Chicken and Vegetable Stir-Fry, 181

Sweet and Spicy Pepper Jelly Chicken and Cauliflower, 165

celery

Buffalo Chicken Salad, 176

Classic Chicken Salad, 176

Cranberry-Almond Chicken Salad, 176

prepping, 25

Waldorf Chicken Salad, 176

cheese

Cheddar-Apple Chicken Burgers, 59

Cheesy Broccoli and Cauliflower Chowder, 150

Chickpea Pizza, 134

Ham, Cheese, and Zucchini Breakfast Quesadillas, 107

Italian Baked Eggs, 175

Lox and Cream Cheese, 173

Mason Jar Instant Lasagna Soup, 74

Pepperoni Pizza Mini Frittatas, 69

Potato Zucchini Muffin Tots, 60

Skillet Turkey Enchiladas, 55

Sloppy Joe–Stuffed Sweet Potatoes, 170

Slow Cooker Four-Veggie Lasagna, 114

"Steak" and Cheese–Stuffed Zucchini, 178

Ultimate Breakfast Scramble, 73

chicken

Barbecue Chicken "Empanadas," 40

Build-Your-Own Chicken Salad, 176

Cashew Chicken and Pineapple Fried Rice, 48

Cheddar-Apple Chicken Burgers, 59

Creamy Ranch Chicken Bites, 118

Creamy Spinach and Artichoke Pasta, 82

Crispy Coconut Chicken Strips, 158

Mason Jar Instant Lasagna Soup, 74

One-Pot Creamy Sausage and Pepper Pasta, 47

Sesame-Orange Chicken and Broccoli, 129

Sheet-Pan Chicken and Vegetable Stir-Fry, 181

Sheet-Pan Pesto Meatballs, Roasted Tomatoes, and Gnocchi, 90

Slow Cooker Honey-Soy Chicken, 77

Slow Cooker Salsa Chicken Chili, 179

Sweet and Spicy Pepper Jelly Chicken and Cauliflower, 165

Ultimate Breakfast Scramble, 73

chicken salad

base, 176

Buffalo, 176

classic, 176

cranberry-almond, 176

curried, 176

Waldorf, 176

chickpeas

Chickpea Pizza, 134

Italian Chopped Salad, 117

Chili, Slow Cooker Salsa Chicken, 179

chocolate

Creamy Chocolate Smoothie, 174

Pumpkin–Chocolate Chip Muffins, 70

Chowder, Cheesy Broccoli and Cauliflower, 150

coconut

Coconut PB&J, 173

Coconut Quinoa, 78

Crispy Coconut Chicken Strips, 158

coleslaw

Blackened Fish Tacos with Mexican Corn Slaw, 130

Crunchy Thai Peanut and Mango Salad, 113

containers, 22

corn

Baked Cilantro-Lime Salmon Packets, 180

Blackened Fish Tacos with Mexican Corn Slaw, 130

Cowboy Caviar, 154

Slow Cooker Salsa Chicken Chili, 179

cornmeal

Crispy Herb Polenta Fries, 52

Lemon-Garlic Roasted Broccoli and Polenta, 94

Cranberry-Almond Chicken Salad, 176

cucumber

Israeli Salad, 44

Mexican Fruit Salad, 98

prepping, 25

Tzatziki, 43

Curried Chicken Salad, 176

D

dressing

kitchen hacks for, 26

prepping, 24

E

edamame: Crunchy Thai Peanut and Mango Salad, 113

eggs

Ham, Cheese, and Zucchini Breakfast Quesadillas, 107

Italian Baked Eggs, 175

Pepperoni Pizza Mini Frittatas, 69

Pesto and Cherry Tomato Frittata, 145

Sheet-Pan Sweet Potato and Veggie Breakfast Hash, 110

Turkey Bacon and Spinach Breakfast Sandwiches, 36

Ultimate Breakfast Scramble, 73

"Empanadas," Barbecue Chicken, 40

Enchiladas, Skillet Turkey, 55

expiration dates, 23

F

family needs, 16–17

fish

Baked Cilantro-Lime Salmon Packets, 180

Blackened Fish Tacos with Mexican Corn Slaw, 130

One-Pan Honey Mustard Salmon, Potatoes, and Broccoli, 56

Tomato-Basil Fish, 93

food preferences, 16

food safety, 22–23

food storage, 20–21, 22–23

food waste, 11, 16

freezing foods, 23

Frittata, Pesto and Cherry, 145

Fruit Salad, Mexican, 98

G

garlic

Crispy Garlic Squash Fries, 169

Garlic Sweet Potato Wedges, 126

kitchen hacks for, 26

Lemon-Garlic Roasted Broccoli and Polenta, 94

prepping, 24

ginger: kitchen hacks for, 26

glass containers, 22

gnocchi: Sheet-Pan Pesto Meatballs, Roasted Tomatoes, and Gnocchi, 90

grains

kitchen hacks for, 26

prepping, 24

storage of, 23

grapes

Curried Chicken Salad, 176

Waldorf Chicken Salad, 176

green beans

    Mini Meatloaves and Green Beans, 125

    prepping, 25

    Sesame-Mandarin Green Beans, 161

grocery shopping tips, 20–21

H

Ham, Cheese, and Zucchini Breakfast Quesadillas, 107

healthyish eating, 9

I

ingredients

    splurge, 21

    substitute, 21

inventory, taking, 21

Israeli Salad, 44

J

jicama: Mexican Fruit Salad, 98

K

kale: Crunchy Thai Peanut and Mango Salad, 113

kitchen hacks, 26

    week 1, 33

    week 2, 67

    week 3, 106

    week 4, 143

L

labeling, 23

lasagna

    Mason Jar Instant Lasagna Soup, 74

    Slow Cooker Four-Veggie Lasagna, 114

leftovers, 18

Lemon-Garlic Roasted Broccoli and Polenta, 94

lentils, Sloppy Joe–Stuffed Sweet Potatoes, 170

lettuce

    Asian Peanut Lettuce Wraps, 162

    Italian Chopped Salad, 117

    prepping, 25

    Simply Yogurt Caesar Salad, 137

Lox and Cream Cheese, 173

lunch, 18

M

mango

    Crunchy Thai Peanut and Mango Salad, 113

    Mango Salsa, 85

meal planning

    benefits of, 11

    grocery shopping tips for, 20–21

    myths, 12–13

    preparing for, 16–17

    template, 182–184

meal prep, 24–25

    week 1, 32–33

    week 2, 66–67

    week 3, 104–105

    week 4, 142–143

meals plans

    digital companion to, 15

    using, 18–20

meatballs, Sheet-Pan Pesto Meatballs, Roasted Tomatoes, and Gnocchi, 90

meatloaf, Mini Meatloaves and Green Beans, 125

meats. See also specific types

    freezing, 20

    storage of, 23

money savings, 11, 12, 21

Muffins, Pumpkin–Chocolate Chip, 70

mushrooms

    Asian Peanut Lettuce Wraps, 162

    Slow Cooker Four-Veggie Lasagna, 114

N

nuts

    Apple-Cinnamon Granola, 146

    Asian Peanut Lettuce Wraps, 162

    Cashew Chicken and Pineapple Fried Rice, 48

    Cranberry-Almond Chicken Salad, 176

    Crunchy Thai Peanut and Mango Salad, 113

O

oats

    Apple-Cinnamon Granola, 146

    Blueberry-Banana Greek Yogurt Pancakes, 39

    Cinnamon Apple and Pear Oatmeal, 109

    Creamy Chocolate Smoothie, 174

    Pumpkin–Chocolate Chip Muffins, 70

    Zucchini Banana Bread Baked Oatmeal, 35

onions

    prepping, 25

    Sheet-Pan Sausage, Potatoes, Peppers, and Onions, 122

organic foods, 21

P

Pancakes, Blueberry-Banana Greek Yogurt, 39

pasta

Creamy Spinach and Artichoke Pasta, 82

kitchen hacks for, 26

Mason Jar Instant Lasagna Soup, 74

One-Pot American Chop Suey, 157

One-Pot Creamy Sausage and Pepper Pasta, 47

Slow Cooker Four-Veggie Lasagna, 114

peanuts

Asian Peanut Lettuce Wraps, 162

Coconut PB&J, 173

Crunchy Thai Peanut and Mango Salad, 113

Pear Oatmeal, Cinnamon Apple and, 109

peas

Cashew Chicken and Pineapple Fried Rice, 48

Sheet-Pan Chicken and Vegetable Stir-Fry, 181

Skillet Pork Tenderloin with Apples and Snap Peas, 89

pepperoni

Baked Pizza Pork Chops with Cauliflower, 51

Pepperoni Pizza Mini Frittatas, 69

peppers

Cashew Chicken and Pineapple Fried Rice, 48

Cowboy Caviar, 154

Crunchy Thai Peanut and Mango Salad, 113

One-Pot American Chop Suey, 157

One-Pot Creamy Sausage and Pepper Pasta, 47

Pineapple Salsa, 153

prepping, 25

Sheet-Pan Sausage, Potatoes, Peppers, and Onions, 122

Skillet Turkey Enchiladas, 55

Sloppy Joe–Stuffed Sweet Potatoes, 170

"Steak" and Cheese–Stuffed Zucchini, 178

pesto

Pesto and Cherry Tomato Frittata, 145

Sheet-Pan Pesto Meatballs, Roasted Tomatoes, and Gnocchi, 90

picky eaters, 13

pineapple

Cashew Chicken and Pineapple Fried Rice, 48

Pineapple Salsa, 153

pinto beans

Shortcut Refried Beans, 133

Skillet Turkey Enchiladas, 55

Slow Cooker Salsa Chicken Chili, 179

pizza

Baked Pizza Pork Chops with Cauliflower, 51

Chickpea Pizza, 134

Pepperoni Pizza Mini Frittatas, 69

polenta

Crispy Herb Polenta Fries, 52

Lemon-Garlic Roasted Broccoli and Polenta, 94

pork

Baked Pizza Pork Chops with Cauliflower, 51

Skillet Pork Tenderloin with Apples and Snap Peas, 89

Slow Cooker Citrus Carnitas with Pineapple Salsa, 153

potatoes. See also sweet potatoes

One-Pan Honey Mustard Salmon, Potatoes, and Broccoli, 56

Potato Zucchini Muffin Tots, 60

Sheet-Pan Pesto Meatballs, Roasted Tomatoes, and Gnocchi, 90

Sheet-Pan Sausage, Potatoes, Peppers, and Onions, 122

Ultimate Breakfast Scramble, 73

poultry, storage of, 23. See also chicken; turkey

prepared meals

prepping, 26

storage of, 23

produce, storage of, 21, 23

proteins, kitchen hacks for, 26

Pumpkin–Chocolate Chip Muffins, 70

Q

Quesadillas, Ham, Cheese, and Zucchini Breakfast, 107

quinoa

Coconut Quinoa, 78

Crunchy Thai Peanut and Mango Salad, 113

R

rice

Cashew Chicken and Pineapple Fried Rice, 48

Cilantro-Lime Cauliflower Rice and Beans, 86

romaine lettuce

Italian Chopped Salad, 117

Simply Yogurt Caesar Salad, 137

S

salads

Build-Your-Own Chicken Salad, 176

Cowboy Caviar, 154

Crunchy Thai Peanut and Mango Salad, 113

Israeli Salad, 44

Italian Chopped Salad, 117

Mexican Fruit Salad, 98

Simply Yogurt Caesar Salad, 137

storage of, 23

salmon

Baked Cilantro-Lime Salmon Packets, 180

One-Pan Honey Mustard Salmon, Potatoes, and Broccoli, 56

salsas

Creamy Salsa Verde, 97

kitchen hacks for, 26

Mango Salsa, 85

Pineapple Salsa, 153

Slow Cooker Salsa Chicken Chili, 179

sauces

kitchen hacks for, 26

prepping, 24

sausage

Blueberry-Maple Breakfast Sausage, 149

Mason Jar Instant Lasagna Soup, 74

One-Pot Creamy Sausage and Pepper Pasta, 47

Sheet-Pan Sausage, Potatoes, Peppers, and Onions, 122

Turkey Sausage and Tortellini Soup, 177

Ultimate Breakfast Scramble, 73

seafood. See also fish

Shrimp Scampi Cakes, 166

storage of, 23

servings

adjusting, 19

number of, 17, 18

shopping list

adding items to, 19–20

sticking to, 21

week 1, 31–32

week 2, 65–66

week 3, 103–104

week 4, 141–142

Shrimp Scampi Cakes, 166

slow cooker meals

Slow Cooker Citrus Carnitas with Pineapple Salsa, 153

Slow Cooker Four-Veggie Lasagna, 114

Slow Cooker Honey-Soy Chicken, 77

Slow Cooker Mediterranean Beef with Tzatziki, 43

Slow Cooker Salsa Chicken Chili, 179

Smoothie, Creamy Chocolate, 174

snap peas, Skillet Pork Tenderloin with Apples and Snap Peas, 89

snow peas, Sheet-Pan Chicken and Vegetable Stir-Fry, 181

soups and stews

Cheesy Broccoli and Cauliflower Chowder, 150

Mason Jar Instant Lasagna Soup, 74

storage of, 23

Turkey Sausage and Tortellini Soup, 177

spices

kitchen hacks for, 26

prepping, 24

spinach

Creamy Chocolate Smoothie, 174

Creamy Spinach and Artichoke Pasta, 82

Pepperoni Pizza Mini Frittatas, 69

Slow Cooker Four-Veggie Lasagna, 114

Turkey Bacon and Spinach Breakfast Sandwiches, 36

Turkey Sausage and Tortellini Soup, 177

Ultimate Breakfast Scramble, 73

splurge ingredients, 21

squash

Crispy Garlic Squash Fries, 169

Roasted Ranch Butternut Squash and Asparagus, 121

Slow Cooker Four-Veggie Lasagna, 114

steak: Broiled Barbecue Flank Steak with Mango Salsa, 85

strawberries: Three-Year-Old Special, 173

substitutions, 21

summer squash

Crispy Garlic Squash Fries, 169

prepping, 25

sweet potatoes

Crispy Baked Sweet Potato Taquitos, 97

Garlic Sweet Potato Wedges, 126

Sheet-Pan Sweet Potato and Veggie Breakfast Hash, 110

Sloppy Joe–Stuffed Sweet Potatoes, 170

T

tacos: Blackened Fish Tacos with Mexican Corn Slaw, 130

time objections, to meal planning, 12

toast: Fancy Toast Five Ways, 173

tofu: Creamy Chocolate Smoothie, 174

tomatoes

Baked Cilantro-Lime Salmon Packets, 180

Cowboy Caviar, 154

Israeli Salad, 44

Italian Chopped Salad, 117

Pesto and Cherry Tomato Frittata, 145

Sheet-Pan Pesto Meatballs, Roasted Tomatoes, and Gnocchi, 90

Tomato-Basil Fish, 93

tortellini: Turkey Sausage and Tortellini Soup, 177

tortillas

Barbecue Chicken "Empanadas," 40

Ham, Cheese, and Zucchini Breakfast Quesadillas, 107

Skillet Turkey Enchiladas, 55

Tots, Potato Zucchini Muffin, 60

turkey

Asian Peanut Lettuce Wraps, 162

Blueberry-Maple Breakfast Sausage, 149

Mini Meatloaves and Green Beans, 125

One-Pot Creamy Sausage and Pepper Pasta, 47

Open Faced BTLA, 173

Sheet-Pan Sweet Potato and Veggie Breakfast Hash, 110

Skillet Turkey Enchiladas, 55

Turkey Bacon and Spinach Breakfast Sandwiches, 36

Turkey Sausage and Tortellini Soup, 177

Tzatziki, 43

V

vegetables. See also specific types

kitchen hacks for, 26

prepping, 24–25

W

Waldorf Chicken Salad, 176

walnuts, Waldorf Chicken Salad, 176

watermelon, Mexican Fruit Salad, 98

week 1, 29

daily tips, 33

game plan, 32–33

kitchen hacks, 33

meal prep, 32–33

shopping list, 31–32

weekly calendar, 30

week 2, 63

daily tips, 67

game plan, 66–67

kitchen hacks, 67

meal prep, 66–67

shopping list, 65–66

weekly calendar, 64

week 3, 101

daily tips, 105

game plan, 104–106

kitchen hacks, 106

meal prep, 104–105

shopping list, 103–104

weekly calendar, 102

week 4, 139

daily tips, 143

game plan, 142–143

kitchen hacks, 143

meal prep, 142–143

shopping list, 141–142

weekly calendar, 140

weekly calendar

week 1, 30

week 2, 64

week 3, 102

week 4, 140

weekly schedule, 16

Y

yogurt

Blueberry-Banana Greek Yogurt Pancakes, 39

Build-Your-Own Chicken Salad, 176

Simply Yogurt Caesar Salad, 137

Tzatziki, 43

Z

zucchini

Ham, Cheese, and Zucchini Breakfast Quesadillas, 107

Mason Jar Instant Lasagna Soup, 74

Potato Zucchini Muffin Tots, 60

prepping, 25

Sheet-Pan Pesto Meatballs, Roasted Tomatoes, and Gnocchi, 90

"Steak" and Cheese–Stuffed Zucchini, 178

Zucchini Banana Bread Baked Oatmeal, 35